BANFF STRIKE WING
AT WAR
A UNIQUE PHOTOGRAPHIC HISTORY

LES TAYLOR

HALSGROVE

To the memory of my grandfather, Alex Barlow

First published in Great Britain in 2010, reprinted 2011

Copyright © Les Taylor 2010

All rights reserved. No part of this publication may be reproduced, stored in a retrieval system, or transmitted in any form or by any means without the prior permission of the copyright holder.

British Library Cataloguing-in-Publication Data
A CIP record for this title is available from the British Library

ISBN 978 0 85704 072 5

HALSGROVE
Halsgrove House,
Ryelands Business Park,
Bagley Road, Wellington, Somerset TA21 9PZ
Tel: 01823 653777   Fax: 01823 216796
email: sales@halsgrove.com

Part of the Halsgrove group of companies
Information on all Halsgrove titles is available at: www.halsgrove.com

Printed and bound in Great Britain by the MPG Books Group

CONTENTS

Acknowledgements	4
Introduction	5
1. The Aim	15
2. The Airfield	33
3. The Men	51
4. The Machines	70
5. The Missions	89
6. The Missing	112
7. The Memory	128
Appendices:	
i. Banff Strike Wing Roll of Honour	146
ii. Ships Sunk by Banff Strike Wing	148
iii. Former Banff Strike Wing Personnel, Correspondence and Interviews	150
Bibliography and Sources	151

ACKNOWLEDGEMENTS

It is fair to say that this wee book has been thirty years in the making.

Along that road there have been many people who helped bring it to fruition, and I would like to take the opportunity to thank a few of them here.

Top of the list must be the man who has done more than anyone to keep the name of RAF Banff alive for well over forty years; journalist, yachtsman and Banffer, David Morgan. Thanks to his endless dynamism and energy, not to mention contacts, a charitable trust was formed in 1987 with the sole aim of building a memorial to Banff Strike Wing. Thanks also go to all our fellow former trustees who achieved the aim with an unveiling ceremony in 1989. They are; Group Captain Angus McIntosh, Doctor William Hossack, Ian Rigby, Alec Robertson and Francie Lamb. Unsung heroes include James McPherson, John Walker and Jimmy Forbes. Special thanks must also go to Colin Jeffrey, who continues to devote enormous efforts to the memory of the Strike Wing through the RAF Banff Association.

The veterans of Banff Strike Wing – naturally – provided the core of the written and photographic material used in this book. To them all, many of whom are sadly no longer with us, I offer my thanks, and hope that I have done your memories and achievements justice. The full list of all those former air and ground crews that I have had the profound pleasure of meeting and corresponding with over the years, is given in the appendices.

Thanks must also go to the families of those who lost their lives flying with Banff Strike Wing, and I am particularly indebted to Bill Atkinson in Australia for the reference material on his father, Wing Commander Richard Atkinson. My old friend Ole Inge Lindaas from Norway has always been a particular tower of strength over the years, and to him and his family I offer my heartfelt thanks for all his help and advice.

Like most writers, I need to give special thanks to my family for their patience. My wife Glenda and my kids Gavin and Kerry, have learned over the years to leave me well alone once I disappear into my room and start tapping away at the keyboard. The nature of the beast means that evenings and weekends are often sadly devoid of their company while I write.

My final acknowledgement however, is a rather less orthodox one.

Like most things in life, it takes a catalyst to spark an interest in any given subject.

In my own case, a lifetime's obsession with RAF Banff came about purely by chance, when I first set foot on the old airfield at Boyndie in 1980 as an eighteen year old on a warm summer night. Although fascinated to see this haunting and desolate place – especially in the spooky half-light of a northern Scottish night in June – my motives on that night had little to do with history and more to do with a blonde called Moira in the passenger seat of my car, who had wickedly lured me to this quiet spot. To her therefore, I must also give due credit for the unwitting introduction.

I like to think that the ghosts of all those young aircrew would have approved.

INTRODUCTION
THE PHOTOGENIC FORCE

TOWARDS THE END OF THE SECOND WORLD WAR, a large multi-squadron force of aircraft operating from an RAF airfield at Banff in north-east Scotland, found itself becoming one of the most filmed and photographed units in the entire history of that war.

There were several reasons why this happened. The most obvious was that by the spring of 1945 the war was clearly almost over. Everyone knew that the momentous scenes of all-out war they were witnessing were never likely to be seen again, and so there was an understandable desire to capture these events on film now that the end was so near.

Secondly, Banff airfield was host to one of the few operational RAF units still fighting the enemy directly from the UK mainland. Access was therefore considerably easier for the average press photographer than to locations overseas, and the enemy was usually far enough away to present little danger during a visit to the station. However, this was a period when the world's eyes were focused on continental Europe and the destruction of Hitler's Third Reich by the advancing Allied forces. Few people were aware that between September 1944 and May 1945, Coastal Command Strike Wings based in north-east Scotland were engaged in intensive air combat over Norway on an almost daily basis. Understandably enough, the RAF was keen to change this and let the world see the important work that their Mosquito and Beaufighter equipped Strike Wings were doing over Norway. Photographs and filmed footage of the action were therefore shot whenever the opportunity arose. Every Banff Strike Wing Mosquito carried a gun camera in the nose, operating automatically whenever the four machine guns next to it opened fire. A hand-held camera was also taken along in the cockpit and operated by the navigator whenever he had time to do so. Every combat the wing took part in thus benefited from a photographic record, all taken on high-quality military cameras. This near-saturation coverage could have put many modern newsrooms to shame. To give an example, on the 30 March 1945, the Mosquito of Flight Lieutenant William Knowles crashed and exploded after hitting power cables during an attack on shipping in Porsgrunn-Skien Harbour. The cameras were all watching, and *at least* a dozen different photographs of the moment of impact are still in existence – some of which appear in this book.

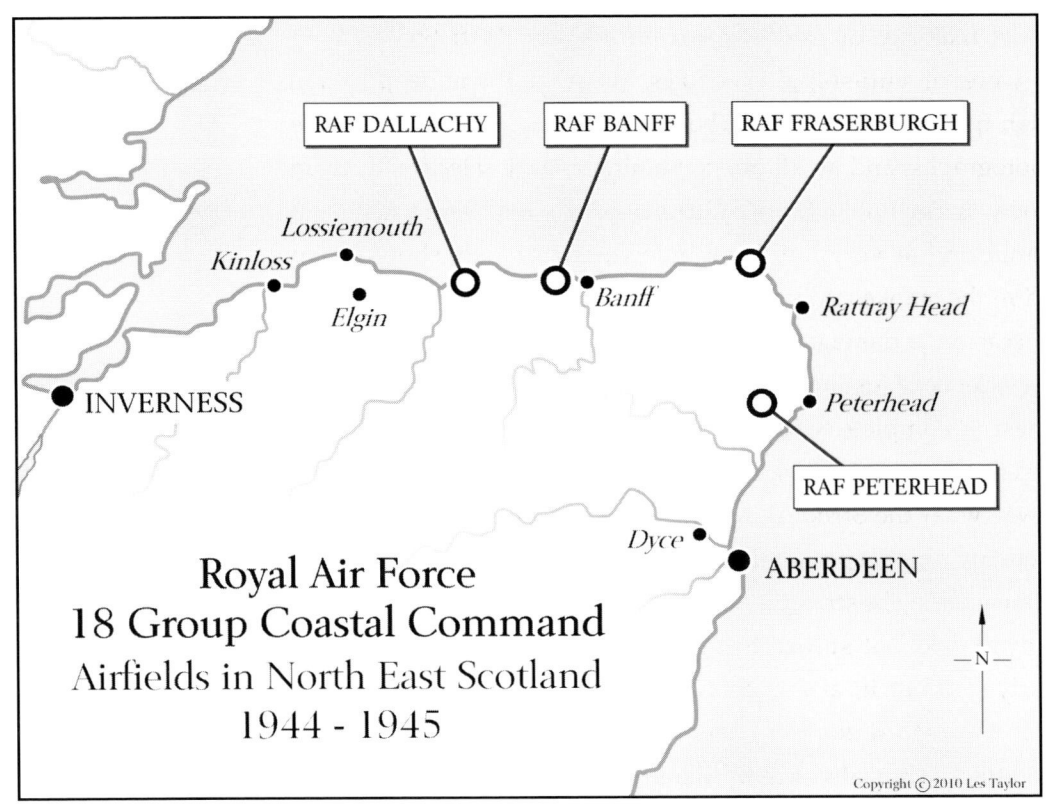

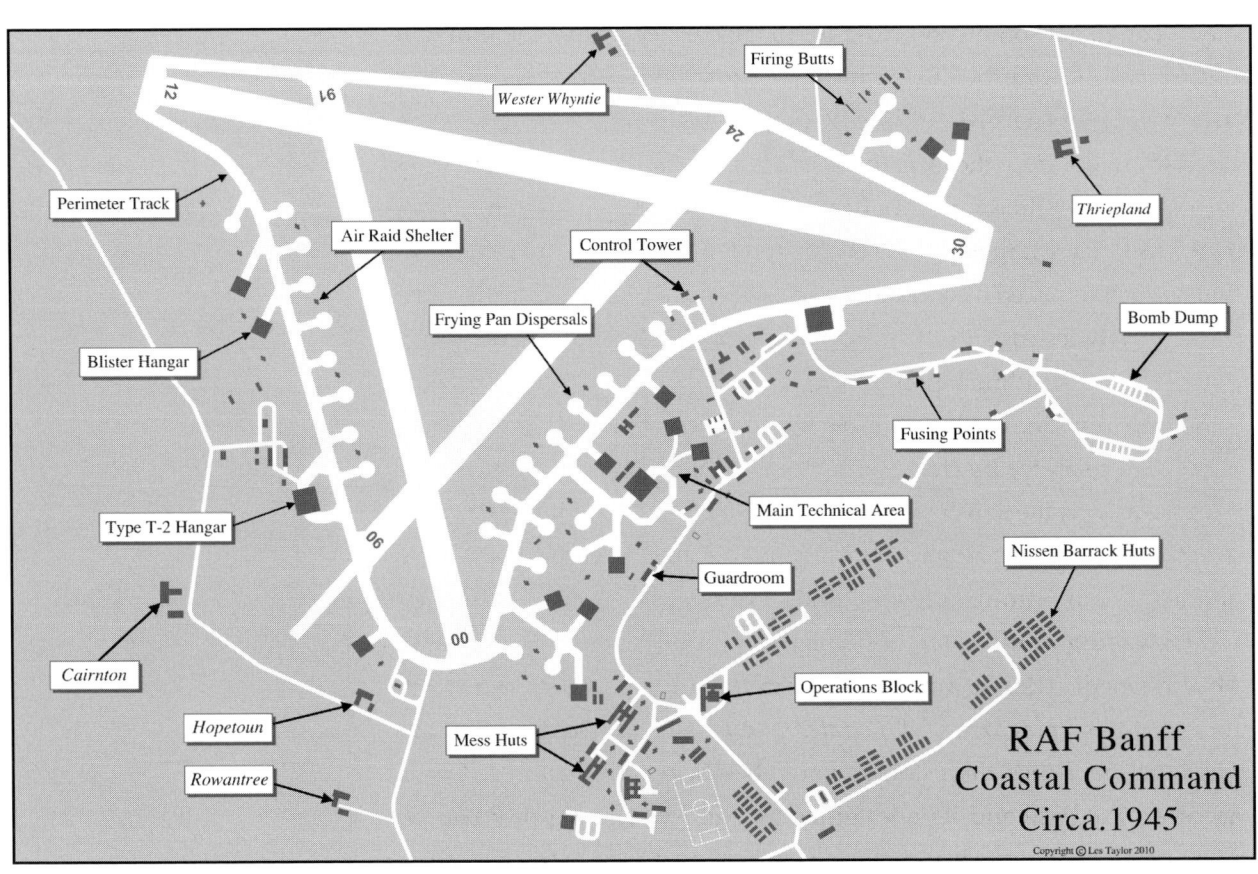

INTRODUCTION

The vast majority of the images captured by Banff Strike Wing cameras were of anti-shipping strikes, most of them deep inside Norwegian fjords and harbours. There are literally hundreds of these strike photographs, and an album containing a large selection of them resides today in the Public Record Office at Kew. They were taken from aircraft attacking at very low level indeed, and usually show a ship wreathed in the smoke and splashes of cannon and rocket fire. On one notable occasion, a damaged Mosquito arrived back at Banff with the physical evidence of just how low it had attacked an enemy vessel. The ship's mast – complete with fluttering red pennant – was firmly embedded in the aircraft's nose.

This was what the Strike Wing was primarily tasked with doing – sinking enemy ships, specifically enemy-operated merchant ships in Norwegian waters. The strategic reasons for this policy will be explained later in this book, but suffice to say that Banff Strike Wing became particularly good at it, and even branched-out in the last couple of months of war into sinking U-boats as well. These were particularly dramatic attacks, but also highly dangerous ones, as the crew of a dedicated RAF Film Unit Mosquito discovered to their cost on the 9 April 1945. The wing had attacked and sunk three U-boats in the Kattegat that day. Keen to get some good close-up footage of the action, the film unit Mosquito followed the attacking aircraft in at very low level, but was then caught in the blast of one of the U-boats when it blew up. The aircraft dived into the sea, killing all aboard. These anti-shipping operations were therefore very hazardous for the aircrew, but they were a vital task. They targeted a key choke-point of the German war machine, and as such required a competent and experienced leader to oversee the mission. Which leads to the third and perhaps most important reason why Banff Strike Wing became so well recorded on film – Max Aitken.

Group Captain, The Honourable Max Aitken, DSO, DFC, was already a national celebrity by the time he took command at Banff, primarily because he was the son of the press baron Lord Beaverbrook and would eventually inherit his father's *Daily Express* newspaper empire. Naturally enough, such strong media connections gave Aitken a unique understanding of the value of publicity - and the contacts to exploit it. The first media team to arrive at Banff in the autumn of 1944 were from the popular magazine, *Illustrated*. Journalist Carl Olsson and photographer James Jarche found themselves being given unprecedented access to the base and its operations by Aitken, who happily laid on staged shoots of aircraft and crews being prepared for battle as well as plenty of strike photographs. *Illustrated* magazine published a large three-

page feature on the Strike Wing in their 1945 edition, under the heading: *FLYERS RAIN DEATH FROM LIMELIT SKY OVER A NIGHT SEA.* The pictures, many in colour (though sadly, none of these colour originals survive), show dramatic scenes on the base and over Norway, and made unnamed stars of some of the airfield personnel. Young WAAF Agnes Shaylor found herself beaming back at the world while holding a rocket projectile over her shoulder, with the caption: *THIS IS THE WAAF WHO*

INTRODUCTION

ADJUSTS THE ROCKETS THAT WORRY THE GERMANS OFF NORWAY.

It was all inspiring stuff, and the ever-popular Aitken ensured that many of the 3,500 strong personnel on his base received either prints of the photographs or copies of the magazine itself. Almost inevitably, next to arrive at Banff was the *Daily Express*. On 4 February 1945, the newspaper ran with the headline: *ROCKET TERROR OF THE FIORDS,* followed by an article that went on to describe the operations – although without naming the airfield or the force that was doing all the terrorising. That was still "classified" information, and even though the German occupation forces in Norway were well aware of where their tormentors were based, the British public could not apparently be trusted with such knowledge. *Flight* magazine also ran an article on the wing and all its flight commanders.

Later in February came a real coup, at least in terms of photography. The noted aviation photographer Charles E. Brown turned up at Banff and was immediately given every opportunity he needed to put the Strike Wing firmly into the pages of history. Armed with the very best cameras and film that money could buy, together with his legendary eye for a good shot, Brown produced a large catalogue of outstanding photographs. On the airfield, number 143 Squadron were put at his disposal and bent over backwards for him. So many superb air-to-air shots of 143 Squadron aircraft were taken in fact, that to this day it seems as if every other photograph of a wartime Mosquito reproduced in print or online is of a 143 Squadron machine, with their distinctive "NE" code letters.

But Max Aitken was far too famous and photogenic a figure to be left out of any shoot, and Brown and the station commander undertook a notable session together. If Banff Strike Wing and the snarling Mosquito aircraft were indeed photogenic, then they were as nothing compared to the love affair the camera had with the dashing Max Aitken. The shoot could not fail to be a winner with such perfect subject matter. First, Aitken taxied his personal red-spinnered Mosquito around the airfield perimeter track for Brown, then stopped the engines and came out to pose in front of his machine which – because he was a Group Captain – was marked with his initials "M-A" instead of a squadron code. Next, Aitken took off, tucked his wheels up quickly in a "fighter-style" take-off, then proceeded to beat up the airfield at low-level for the famous photographer below.

Armed with the latest Kodak Eastman colour film Brown captured a superb series of photographs that day, the sharpness, clarity and depth of which make them look as if they had been taken only yesterday. The entire collection now resides at the RAF Museum in Hendon.

But there were other photographers at work at Banff as well, mostly individual servicemen shooting off a snap here and there, as well as the station's Intelligence Officer, George Bellew, a world-famous heraldic artist by civilian trade who also had an eye for a good picture. Yet when it comes to the single most important photograph ever snapped at Banff, there seems to be no record of who took it, nor where the original

INTRODUCTION

negative nor even a print may reside to this day. There is a copy negative, but that's all. Beyond all doubt however, is the sheer atmosphere of that now famous picture.

The *Taxi Rank* photograph – shown on the previous pages – was taken from the roof of the control tower at Banff and is a picture that has come to be regarded as a classic wartime image. Often described as the best photograph ever taken of a British airfield at war, author David Smith most accurately describes the photograph in his *Action Stations* volume about Scottish airfields as "reeking of atmosphere".

And so it does. Taken in April or May 1945, it shows a line of rocket-armed Mosquitoes threading their way up the perimeter track past the control tower to the runway before another strike mission. In the background is one of the few panoramic scenes ever taken of a typical wartime "austerity" airfield. Built urgently during the depths of total war, equipped with only temporary huts and aircraft hangars, these utilitarian airfields were designed to be "disposable" and were all unceremoniously abandoned as soon as hostilities had ended. That's why this picture is such a masterpiece of opportunistic photography, taken by someone who, seeing what may perhaps have been a mundane everyday scene to them, shoots off a frame to let the world share a moment in time that would never be seen again.

Banff Strike Wing and the airfield it operated from were therefore particularly well photographed and recorded. Yet both became relatively forgotten about in the decades after the war ended, although it is not too hard to understand why. The Banff Strike Wing story took place far away from the "main events" on the soil of France and Germany, and when it came to telling war stories, there was a lot of competition around in the immediate post-war decades.

Pop-culture history was soon being led by Paul Brickhill, who in the 1950s began to feed the British public with stirring tales of great wartime exploits. Thanks to Brickhill, *The Dambusters* soon became a household name, as did *The Great Escape* and *Reach for the Sky*. Unfortunately, the closest that Banff Strike Wing ever came to receiving similar treatment was at the hands of a 1956 novel entitled *633 Squadron* by Frederick E. Smith, together with a follow-up movie of the same name. On balance, although the film was a visual treat with all those Mosquitoes and a stirring soundtrack, the plot and the acting were so dire that it was perhaps a blessing that Smith never actually named Banff as the influence for his story.

But at least this left the history of the wing in the hands of serious historians. In the 1970s, the great Chaz Bowyer began to plant enough seeds in his superb illustrated history books to keep the name alive, and to tease a younger generation like this writer with some of the many photographs that were available of Banff Strike Wing. One of these of course was the *Taxi Rank* photograph. What really kindled my childhood interest in this picture however, was Chaz Bowyer's mention of the name Banff and the rather surprising revelation that – despite the common misconception that northern Scotland was a wartime backwater – this famous image had been captured only a few miles from where I lived.

The catalyst created in my childhood by Chaz Bowyer and that wonderful photograph eventually helped set the ball rolling in 1987, with the creation of a local charitable trust dedicated to building a memorial to Banff Strike Wing, which was successfully unveiled in September 1989. Having come up with the idea in the first place, I was given the dubious reward of being elected secretary and treasurer of the trust. But this had some distinct advantages, and photographs – as always – were the key. Suddenly, names from the pages of all those history books were getting in touch with me – pilots from 235 and 248 Squadrons, navigators from 143 Squadron and ground crewmen from 333 Squadron – all pouring out their memories on paper for me. All of them had written to donate some cash to the memorial project, but they also donated those other magical ingredients as well – photographs.

It was the veritable avalanche of photographs (together with other personal memorabilia and keepsakes) that were donated to us, that really brought home how comprehensively the Strike Wing had been photographed during that last year of war. Twenty years after the memorial was unveiled and the trust set up to achieve that goal was disbanded, I still have all those photographs and documents. For years, they have taunted me from within their storage boxes to finally getting round to doing something with them. Inevitably, they were always going to have the final say, and this book is the result.

One thing I was determined this book would *not* be though, was a long and laborious diary of Banff Strike Wing operations. A major by-product of the media attention our memorial project created, was a sea-change in interest in this relatively unexplored subject. As a result, there are now enough works of reference about the wing to satisfy even the most demanding of readers regarding dates and places, and they are listed at the end of this book.

Perhaps it was because of the personal contact I've had with so many of the Strike Wing veterans over the years, as well as the fact that Banff airfield is a well-explored local place for me, rather than somewhere distant I have never visited, that made me so determined that this book

INTRODUCTION

would not simply be a procession of bare facts. In contrast, I decided I would use my collection to provide an up-close and personal picture of Banff Strike Wing in the form of a photographic history, because there is nothing quite like a photograph to tell a story.

Or even perhaps, to hook the interest of the next generation...

Although many of these photographs have been in print before and are available from official sources, most of them have never previously been published. All of the photographs used in this book have been scanned in high resolution directly from the original wartime prints donated to the trust or to me personally by veterans or their families. All have also had a wee digital wash and brush-up to remove scratches and blemishes as well.

In addition, I thought it would be a nice way of emphasising the human nature of the subject matter by making use of a collection of 235 Squadron magazines donated by former 235 pilot David "Jack" Frost. Although little more than stapled photocopies of typewritten pages, these were packed with the sort of gossipy quips and station anecdotes so beloved of service personnel during wartime. I have therefore included many examples of the short, snappy observations and cutting one-liners from these magazines, in order to give a true picture of the humour, warmth and optimism of this remarkable wartime generation.

This book is therefore a unique photographic record of Banff Strike Wing, and it is unique for one particular reason. These photographs are the former keepsakes and treasured snapshots of the people who either took the pictures themselves, or who appear in them. In many cases, they are the last image of a loved one: a timeless picture of a friend, or a relative, or a husband, looking back out of a photograph at us - shortly before he was killed in action.

Some even show the moment of death of these brave young men.

This book is, therefore, not only a picture of Banff Strike Wing at war, it is also a picture of the *people* who took it to war.

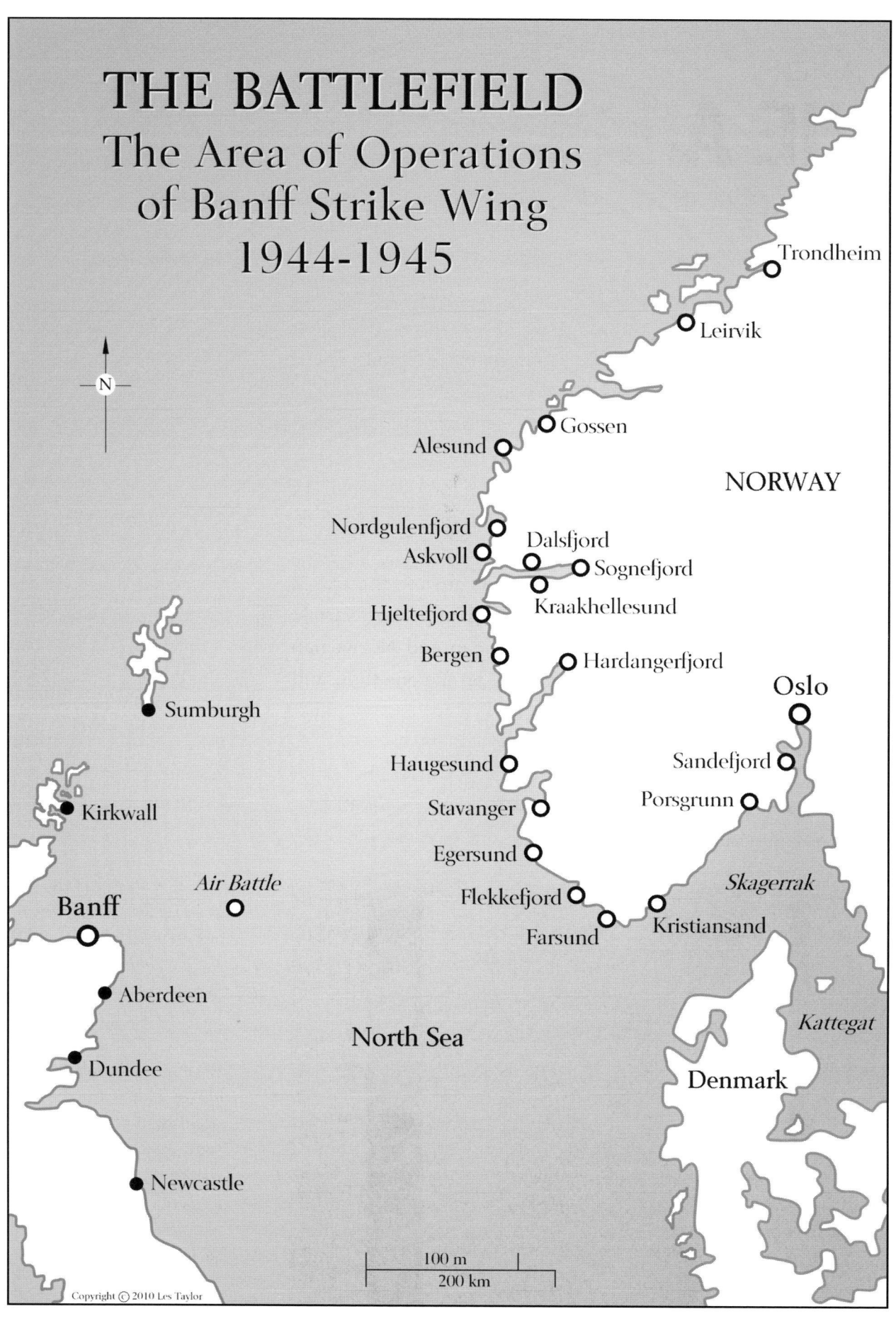

CHAPTER 1
THE AIM

THE ROLE OF BANFF STRIKE WING can be summed up in a single word – steel. Without steel, no nation in the twentieth century could sustain a war for any period of time. Tanks, ships, submarines, aircraft engines – all the weapons and tools of modern war required steel in vast quantities. If steel is that important, then so too is the raw material to make it – iron ore. Germany's main source of high grade iron ore has always been Sweden. Ore from here is hard to transport to the blast furnaces and steel mills of the Ruhr valley however, since the Swedish ore mines are in the far north of the country. The only viable route was to take the ore via a mountain rail link to the northern Norwegian port of Narvik. From here, a dedicated fleet of both German and Norwegian merchant ships would set off with the ore on the one-thousand mile voyage to the ports of northern Germany, returning with their holds full of German coal.

This lucrative arrangement worked fine in peacetime, but it did not take a degree in economics to see that in a wartime situation, this trade route had the potential to be one of Germany's key weak

The ultimate aim: This unidentified merchant ship lies partially sunk in the shallows of a Norwegian fjord after being attacked by Banff Strike Wing. The original caption in David Frost's personal photo album states – The occasional proof that they did sometimes sink. By the end of the war, Norwegian fjords and harbours were littered with such highly visible proof.

The Shining Sword: The ultimate configuration of the anti-shipping version of the De Havilland Mosquito FBVI, that was unique to Banff Strike Wing and it's operations. In addition to the already formidable armament of cannon and machine guns, this battle-stained aircraft carries two pairs of tiered rockets and a large paper-mache fuel drop tank under each wing. This 143 Squadron aircraft, coded NE-D, would be lost with its crew in a big air battle with German fighters over Leirvik in January 1945.

We mean business: One of the earliest arrivals at the Strike Wing's new base was this Airspeed Oxford utility aircraft. Ironically, the arrival of the Strike Wing had caused the eviction of number 14(Pilot) Advanced Flying Unit, a large Oxford-equipped training unit. The badge on the nose gives a clue to the serious intentions of the RAF when it came to publicising their new wing. Rather incredibly, the letters stand for Coastal Command Public Relations.

spots. Before war broke out, Fritz Thyssen, a German steel-maker and ardent anti-Nazi, sent London a memo pointing out his conviction that whoever either controlled the iron ore deposits in Sweden, or their transit route through Northern Norway, would win the war. With Hitler and Churchill well aware of this, both saw the same solution to the matter – invade and occupy Norway. Hitler naturally wanted to guarantee his supplies of iron ore, so that Germany could continue to make all the tanks and guns she would need to fight a long war, while Churchill saw a golden opportunity to cut off this supply completely. It was why Hitler successfully invaded Norway in 1940, and why Churchill unsuccessfully tried to do the same thing at Narvik at more or less the same time.

The vital strategic importance of German iron ore supplies was therefore recognised by both sides right from the start of the war. But it was not the only raw material that Germany needed to import (and in vast quantities) to survive. The other was crude oil. During the Great War, Germany had been weakened to the point of near collapse by the British naval blockade of her ports. Clearly, a similar blockade of her raw material imports was bound to have a dramatic and rapid effect on her ability to wage war in this conflict as well.

But this war was already proving to be very different from the last one. From 1940 onwards, as Nazi Germany expanded her conquered territories, raw materials became less of an issue as supplies became available from these new sources – particularly the rich pickings to be had in the Soviet Union. It was not until the high-water mark of Stalingrad, followed by the long and brutal retreat back towards her own borders, that Germany's dependence on imported raw materials once more became a key strategic issue for her. She was still able to obtain some stocks from the mines in

"CLUELESS CROSS"

The Ancient Moronic Society of Clueless Clots has graciously approved the award of the Order of the Clueless Cross to Sgt . . . . . ., for Amazing Lack of Observation. This sergeant, on finishing his day's duties, rushed out of his flight office, mounted his bicycle, gave it full boost and carried out the neatest ground-loop three yards ahead of the bicycle, still clutching the handlebars, which had been parted from the parent unit in no uncertain manner. The rope attaching the rear forks to the cycle shed was proved to be even stronger than the language of the owner of the machine, W/O Bussey, when it was returned to him sans handlebars.

Chocks Away, October 1944

Achieving the aim: Two Norwegian Home Fleet ships have been caught by Banff Strike Wing in Sandefjord on 2 April 1945 and are being raked by cannon fire. These merchant ships, commandeered by the Germans, carried vital iron ore from Sweden via Narvik to Germany for the steel mills of the Ruhr. In this photograph, the 3,604 ton William Blumer *is nearest the camera and about to be sunk. The 5,742 ton* Hektor *behind her was saved from the same fate by the close proximity of the* Blumer *and was only damaged, although this put her in dock for repairs for several weeks. The* William Blumer *was raised in 1946 and sailed on until 1956, when she finally ran aground near Ceylon, ironically while carrying a cargo of iron ore.*

Not for the faint-hearted: Ship-busting was a dangerous business for all concerned. The key to sinking merchant ships was to get in as close as possible and pepper the hull with cannon fire and rockets – preferably below the waterline. The ship under attack here is the 3,323 ton Iris. *At least five flak gun cupolas can be seen on her deck. She was sunk in this attack in Alesund on the 17 of March 1945, along with two other ships, the 1,830 tone* Remage, *and the 1,684 ton* Log. *In balance, two Mosquitoes were shot down by Flak, with one crew killed and the other – including strike leader Roy Orrock - being captured.*

THE AIM

north-eastern France and Belgium, but following the D-Day invasion of June 1944 and – much more importantly – the armoured break-out from Normandy, the situation regarding the supply of iron ore to Germany changed dramatically. From then on, only the Swedish lifeline was keeping the blast furnaces of the Ruhr supplied with steel, and the new chief of Coastal Command was quick to recognise the opportunity.

Air Chief Marshal Sir Sholto Douglas was appointed head of Coastal Command in time for the D-Day invasion, and used the increasing strength of his anti-shipping Strike Wings to great effect in support of the invasion. These Strike Wings had begun to make their mark operating from coastal airfields such as Portreath in Cornwall and North Coates in Lincolnshire. Earlier in the war, the aircraft and weaponry available for such operations were poor and in short supply, but gradually the Bristol Beauforts began to be replaced with the much more capable Bristol Beaufighter, and in larger numbers. By the time Sholto Douglas took command, these Beaufighters were in turn beginning to be superseded by the even more capable Coastal Command version of the De Havilland Mosquito FBVI.

By August 1944, the American USAAF was going after Germany's raw materials with a vengeance and hitting crude oil refineries in places like Ploesti in Romania. Soon, these oil attacks would start having very dramatic effects, with German aircraft grounded, Panzer tanks stranded on the battlefields, and road transport reduced to horses and carts – all for lack of fuel. Synthetic oil was produced in Germany from coal by the IG Farbern cartel,

Man with a mission: It was vital that a strong leader with a proven background be placed in charge of the new Strike Wing's operations. Few people fitted the bill better than 34-year old Group Captain Max Aitken, DSO, DFC, who had cut his teeth in air combat back in the Battle of Britain and had been fighting ever since. Aitken was a multiple "ace" with 14 enemy aircraft "kills" to his name. Here, "Bayhound Leader" poses in front of his personal red-spinnered Mosquito on the northern perimeter track beside Wester Whyntie Farm for the camera of Charles E. Brown in late February 1945.

> **"WELCOME"**
> In charge of the Squadron now is W/Cdr. R. A. Atkinson, DSO, DFC, a man of few words and much experience. He had a fine record before joining our Wing and if Jerry presents the opportunities he will enhance it during the future. We all have the utmost confidence in him and believe that under his leadership the Squadron will move on to greater deeds.
> *Chocks Away, November 1944*

Cold comfort: In order to reassure aircrew faced with coming down in the North Sea, the air-dropped lifeboat was developed. Vickers Warwick aircraft from a detachment of 281 Squadron based at Banff would follow the wing and drop these lifeboats to crews forced to ditch in the sea. Sometimes they even worked. Among the men posing for a press photograph here, is the young American pilot Frederick Alexandre of 143 Squadron, who would be shot down and killed in a dogfight with nine FW-190 fighters over Leirvik in January 1945.

Porsgrunn-Skien: The scene at a typical busy Norwegian quayside on the 30 March 1945, when Banff Strike Wing paid a visit. Here, one of the five large merchant ships sunk that day is attacked right on the quayside. Port facilities and personnel obviously suffered indirectly from overshooting cannon and rocket fire as a result of such close-quarter attacks. The distinctive-roofed warehouse at the bottom of the picture survives to this day.

THE AIM

No safe havens: The 3,215 ton Norwegian merchant ship Belpamela *under attack while in the floating dry dock* Kabel. *Although she could not technically be sunk, she was badly damaged. Since the destruction of enemy-held merchant shipping was the primary objective of Banff Strike Wing, it was vital that the use of Norway's extensive ship repair facilities were also denied to the occupying German forces. This attack on the yard of the company A/S Framnaes Mekaniske Verksted in Sandefjord took place on the 2 April 1945. Flak bursts can clearly be seen near an attacking Mosquito. Almost exactly two years later, the repaired* Belpamela *foundered off Newfoundland with a cargo of sixteen railway locomotives.*

Hitting the Harbours: After the Norwegian Home Fleet stopped all daytime sailings to avoid attacks at sea, Banff Strike Wing was given little option other than to attack shipping inside fjords and harbours. Here, on the 11 April 1945, Porsgrunn-Skien is again the target, and several Mosquitoes are attacking at the same time in this photograph. Rockets streak toward the ship in the centre, while it would appear from the sudden release of steam that the ship on the left has had its boilers damaged. Four ships were sunk in this attack, the Dione, *the* Kalmar, *the* Nordsjo *and the* Traust, *with two other ships badly damaged. One Mosquito was shot down by German fighters during this attack, with both of the 333 Squadron crew killed.*

The top brass take a look: Pictured in front of an Avro Anson transport aircraft at Banff with Max Aitken, the AOC of number 18 Group of Coastal Command based at Pitreavie in Fife was the highly experienced Air Vice Marshal S.P. Simpson. Much to the dismay of his superiors at 18 Group, Max Aitken was never a great stickler for formal dress codes, and proudly stands here with his tunic button undone. Usually, he never even wore a tie.

but this was a particularly poor substitute and was soon being targeted by the bombers as well. That left steel as the other strategic raw material requiring interdiction, and an increasingly powerful Coastal Command were more than ready for the challenge. The action would all take place over Norway, and so it was time for the bulk of Coastal Command to move north. It has been suggested that Banff Strike Wing was created in order to deal with the enforced relocation of German U-boats from their bases in western France (by now overrun by Patton and his tanks) to northern Germany, but this welcome opportunity to sink some of the hated U-boats was merely an unexpected by-product of the effort to cut the iron ore supplies.

Two Coastal Command airfields were available in north-east Scotland – Banff and Dallachy – providing ideal bases for two new Strike Wings to operate from. During September and October 1944, the Beaufighters and Mosquitos began to take up residence at these bases. Four or five squadrons were based at Banff at any one time, with two or three at the smaller satellite of Dallachy, near Buckie. Their task was a simple one – sink the iron ore-carrying ships, and cut off the only remaining supply of this strategic raw material to Germany.

Sinking these ships was to have a more dramatic effect that is perhaps realised. For one thing, Germany was now under a maritime blockade and unlike the Allies, was in no position to replace any shipping losses she suffered. Once a ship was sunk, there was nothing available to take its place. The iron ore fleet had always consisted of both German and Norwegian merchant ships. Following the German invasion of Norway in 1940, those ships of the huge Norwegian merchant fleet that had not escaped and fallen into German hands, became known as the Norwegian Home Fleet. Although still mostly crewed by Norwegian sailors, they

> **"IN FEAR AND TREMBLING"**
> Which corporal tried to uncouple the coaches on a recent train journey from Aberdeen? And who was found later the same day clutching a goal-post and yelling "They shall not pass!"? And who picketed the hut down because it was rocking too much?
> *Chocks Away, Xmas Edition, December 1944*

THE AIM

Hit anything that floats: Although this small merchant vessel would appear harmless, the presence of a Flak gun cupola on the bow gives the game away. All merchant shipping in Norwegian waters were considered to be in German hands and therefore liable to be attacked. Here, the low-flying Mosquito is using it's nose machine guns to "walk" its fire to the target before loosing its cannons and rockets. Glowing white-hot shrapnel fills the airspace that the attacking Mosquito is about to fly through.

The hated Grey Wolves: Toward the end of the war, German U-boats began to be encountered on the surface more frequently by Banff Strike Wing and were attacked without mercy. The wing sunk no less than five U-boats in April 1945 and damaged another two. In this attack on the 19 April, U-521 was sunk and U-2335 damaged. The 143 Squadron Mosquito in this picture has itself only narrowly avoided being hit by a chunk of flying shrapnel.

Hard to hit: This photograph shows two of the four German merchants ships of the Hamburg-Amerika Line *attacked in Nordgulenfjord on the 5 December 1944. All the ships were moored through the day close against the steep sides of the fjord and only sailed in the safety of darkness. It seems to have saved them. None of the four ships –* Ostland, Tucuman *(built in Greenock),* Magdalena *and* Helene Russ *- were sunk. Flak positioned high in the sides of the fjord hit the Wing hard, however. One 248 Squadron Mosquito was shot down, one crashed at Sumburgh and eight others were badly damaged.*

Little friends: Initially, strikes over Norway were a carefully co-ordinated affair involving torpedo-armed Beaufighters, together with rocket-firing Mosquitoes, all escorted by P-51 Mustang fighters from RAF Peterhead. All would rendezvous over Rattray Head lighthouse before heading out over the North Sea in a massive display of firepower. Here, a 404 Squadron Beaufighter still wears its D-Day "invasion stripes" as it meets up with one of the 315 (Polish) Squadron Mustang escorts over northern Aberdeenshire in September 1944.

THE AIM

A show of force: This 18-ship Mosquito formation passes from east to west over the control tower at RAF Banff for the benefit of the camera of Illustrated *magazine photographer James Jarche in October 1944. Although undoubtedly an impressive sight and sound, this formation was perhaps only one-third of the size of the average force that would assemble over Banff before a typical strike. Such effective and overwhelming firepower was simply not available to Coastal Command in the first few years of the war.*

were under the direct control of the German armed forces, and directly serving Nazi Germany by ensuring her Swedish iron ore needs continued to be met. These Norwegian ships, along with the German merchantmen, were soon fitted with as many deck-mounted anti-aircraft guns as they could carry. This key modification meant that they were no longer innocent merchant ships – they were armed fighting ships, and therefore legitimate targets. Despite this fact, huge Norwegian flags were painted on to the hulls of these ships by the Germans, in the vain hope that Coastal Command might leave them alone.

It was a cynical and fraudulent ploy, but it did not work. It is true that many innocent Norwegian lives were lost as a direct result of Strike Wings attacks, both on the ships that were sunk and in harbours and shipyards. But most Norwegians (though not all of them), accepted that this was a necessary price to pay in order to be liberated. Civilian casualties incurred accidentally during Strike Wing attacks were still a far cry from the effects of the big Allied bombing attacks that were still being launched without mercy on cities like Dresden. Besides, many of the Strike Wing aircraft doing the attacking wore highly visible Norwegian colours painted on their propeller spinners, and this clear presence of free Norwegians operating from the UK was a real morale booster for the population of occupied Norway.

It should also be noted that the Strike Wings (and especially their long-range Mustang escorts) achieved another unexpected result with their determined and relentless operations over Norway – the contest and command of Norwegian skies. Even today, few people realise just how powerful the German occupying forces were in

BANFF STRIKE WING AT WAR

Collateral damage: This attack at Alesund in the half-light of a northern winter sky, shows why strikes on harbours regularly caused casualties among innocent civilians onshore. But not all were innocent. The large building nearest the ships was a hotel being used as barracks for German soldiers, while the timber yard in front of it was owned by what was reputed to be a local "Quisling". It burned out of control for two days after this attack.

Norway, especially by the end of the war, when it began to look as if there may be a more sinister reason for this. While the Luftwaffe based in Germany had become something of an impotent force by the last year of war, starved as it was both of fuel and of experienced pilots, the German armed forces based in Norway remained very powerful, well-equipped and with many highly experienced aces manning the newest fighter aircraft. Even the latest secret jet aircraft were relocated to Norway near the end of the fighting. There was an increasingly realistic fear that Hitler and his Nazis might even be prepared to mount a dramatic last stand in Norway. During those last nine months of the war, Banff and Dallachy Strike Wings took absolute command of both the sea and the skies over Norway, and forced the German occupiers to accept that there could be no Wagnerian last stand in Norway, any more than there could be in the mountains of Bavaria.

The order given to the Strike Wings was therefore a fair and valid one – attack and sink anything in Norwegian waters that floats. This policy was made clear to the Norwegian people by their own government in exile. There would be civilian casualties, but this was war and the task of the Strike Wings was a vital strategic one. Unfortunate incidents such as the attack on the merchant vessel *Austri* on the 21 February 1945, in which 30 Norwegian civilians were killed, were regrettable. But far worse was happening, far more often, and on a far greater scale in other theatres of this terrible war. On the whole, the Strike Wings fought a clean war, and any criticism levelled at them for incidents like the *Austri* is totally unwarranted.

THE AIM

After the battle: It is often hard to equate some of the present day scenes in the tranquil and picturesque coastal towns of south-western Norway where the Strike Wing attacks took place, with the scenes of such wartime violence that the old strike photographs portray. Here is the same location in Alesund today, with the quayside hotel now notable only by its absence.

A big battlefield: The scale of Banff Strike Wing's area of operations is evident from the main map in the Operations Block at RAF Banff. Here, Max Aitken briefs aircrew before a strike. The wartime censor seems to have been very conscientious, obliterating almost every written word visible on the original negative. Some of the markings on these blackboards can still be seen on the walls of this near-derelict building to this day.

Besides, the shipping strikes in Norway quickly achieved a tangible and far-reaching strategic effect. As soon as the wings at Banff and Dallachy got into their stride in the autumn of 1944, the Germans put a complete stop to daytime sailings, and only moved their iron ore shipments in the safety of darkness. Traditionally, they had sailed day and night on the long voyage from northern Norway down the "leads" (the huge collection of offshore islands scattering the west coast of Norway). As soon as this daytime sailing ban came into force, the journey time to Germany (and back) was effectively doubled, and it is important to point out that this single factor alone had an *immediate* effect on German steel production.

Both the British and Americans conducted post-war surveys to determine the effectiveness (or not) of the mass bombing raids, and the report entitled *The Strategic Air War Against Germany 1939-1945*, published by the British Bombing Survey Unit, makes this telling observation on page 88 of their final report:

German officials such as Speer, Saur and Kehrl, are practically unanimous in the opinion that the supply of raw materials was fully adequate for essential programmes up to the second half of 1944.

THE AIM

Not as innocent as it looks: While the policy of attacking any ship afloat in Norwegian waters was militarily justified, it could often appear harsh. This vessel has been raked by gunfire and a tracer round is streaking towards it. But closer inspection reveals – in addition to the crew's washing hanging out on the deck - two guns on the forecastle and one at the stern.

Gather the best: By November 1944, when this photograph was taken, Station Commander Max Aitken had certainly done that, when he posed with his various Squadron Commanders at RAF Banff. Every RAF man in the picture wears at least a DFC ribbon on his uniform. From left to right, they are: W/Cdr. E.H. "Sam" McHardy, 143 Sqn; W/Cdr. G.D. "Bill" Sise, 248 Sqn; Major Egil Johanssen, 333 Sqn; Gp/Cpt. Max Aitken; W/Cdr. A.A. "Dick" Atkinson, 235 Sqn; W/Cdr. R.H. McConnel, 248 Sqn; W/Cdr. "Maurice", 143 Sqn.

Any way we have to: The defensive measure taken by the Norwegian and German fleet of mooring against the steep sides of fjords during daytime, often prevented beam-on attacks and Strike Wing aircraft therefore had to fly perilously close to the sides of the fjords to attack their targets from the stern or the bows. Here, two moored merchantmen are given a lesson in outstanding airmanship by the determined crew of an attacking Mosquito.

Why the second half of 1944? The efforts of Bomber Command to destroy German industry and its sources of supply and materials had being going on since 1942, yet had not achieved anywhere near such a spectacular reduction – in fact quite the reverse. The industrial infrastructure of the Ruhr was hammered on many occasions by Bomber Command, and yet steel production (as well as all other forms of production) continued to rise throughout it all. Besides, by summer 1944, attacks on German cities had been temporarily halted in favour of supporting the D-Day invasion. Furthermore, the steel mills of the Ruhr were not overrun by the advancing western allies until well into 1945.

So why did, as the report so clearly states, German raw material supply fall away so dramatically in the second half of 1944? So much emphasis has always been put on what Bomber Command might or might not have done to German industry, yet the clear evidence is there in the report that when the Coastal Command Strike Wings finally began to put the squeeze on Germany's only remaining source of iron ore, the strategy had an immediate and profound effect on German industry – something that Coastal Command have never been given proper credit for amid all the ballyhoo about Bomber Command's activities.

As can be seen, it was not even necessary for the Strike Wings to sink any ships to achieve such a drastic reduction of iron ore supplies – but sinking as many of them as possible could only add to Germany's woes. Initially, the tactic was to employ a combined set-piece attack involving all the forces that were available in

THE AIM

north-east Scotland. Beaufighters would approach merchant shipping convoys at low-level and attack them with torpedoes. The Mosquitos would simultaneously dive down and suppress the flak from the ships with their cannon and rocket fire, while P-51 Mustang fighters from RAF Peterhead would provide top cover against enemy fighters. It worked too, right up until the moment the Germans put a complete ban on daytime sailings. From then on, the tactics had to change, but by then it was clear that one weapon above all others was sufficient for the job – the rocket.

Wing-mounted rockets were found to be perfectly capable of sinking the relatively thin-skinned merchant ships by themselves, and by the time the iron ore ships took to holing-up deep inside fjords and harbours during the day, attacking them with cannon and rocket fire was the only option left to the Strike Wings anyway. It had to be done at low-level, and was therefore very hazardous since even light anti-aircraft fire (universally known by its German acronym of *Flak*) could be brought to bear against the attacking aircraft. The trouble with light flak, is that it is far more murderous than it sounds. 37mm flak guns were the standard issue on merchant shipping in German service in Norway, and together with quadruple 20mm flak mountings, could hose down the sky in front of low-flying Strike Wing aircraft. The casualty rate among the Strike Wings was therefore high, and few attacks came away unscathed.

As each month went past, tactics and weaponry improved. Spotting ships and convoys was a job undertaken by a detached flight of number 333 (Norwegian) Squadron based at Banff, who would then act as "out-riders", guiding the wing in to wherever they had spotted a likely target. These single aircraft soon became known as the harbingers of doom all over Norway, and the appearance of one was usually enough to put flak gunners on full alert, ready and waiting for the inevitable strike. Alerted too, were the German fighters. Messerschmitt Bf-109 fighters, together with the highly potent Focke-Wulf Fw-190, often flown by very experienced and decorated German *Experten* fighter pilots, pounced regularly and effectively time and again on Strike Wing attacks, causing steady losses. Although a Mosquito could deliver a ferocious barrage of fire against the average German fighter, it was inevitably not as nimble as a single-engine fighter, and but for the presence of RAF P-51 Mustang escort fighters tackling the enemy fighters as well, Strike Wing losses might well have been even higher than they were. But despite the ferocious fire from the flak gunners and the fighter pilots, the Germans were fighting a losing battle against the RAF Mosquitos, Beaufighters and Mustangs. Eventually, the Strike Wings began to run out of targets to hit, with every fjord and harbour soon becoming choked with wrecked and partially sunken merchant ships.

In the end, the Banff and Dallachy Strike Wings had sunk over 100,000 tons of merchant shipping in Norwegian waters, and damaged almost as much again during the short nine month period of their operational life. They destroyed port and repair facilities all over Norway, and brought seaborne traffic in western Scandinavia almost to a complete standstill.

More importantly, they had effectively cut off the supply of Swedish iron ore to the steel mills of Nazi Germany. This had been the sole aim of the Strike Wings based in north-east Scotland. In retrospect, it may seem like an ambitious strategic objective to have given to such a relatively small force. Rather remarkably however, it was precisely what they achieved.

CHAPTER 2
THE AIRFIELD

IF BANFF STRIKE WING deserves a unique place in wartime history, then surely so too does the place that gave the Wing its illustrious name – RAF Banff. Yet what gives the story of the airfield such poignancy is the fact that this anonymous coastal hillside has never looked anything even remotely illustrious. Neither was it intended to. Royal Air Force Station, Banff, was specifically created as a disposable airfield, a tool conceived in the depths of total war, equipped with only the most basic of necessities to do the job, designed to be abandoned and forgotten as soon as that job had been done. And abandoned she indeed was, quickly and unceremoniously – and almost forgotten into the bargain.

Yet it is this very utilitarian appearance of RAF Banff, with the sea of tin huts visible in so many of the photographs taken there,

Taking shape: The almost completed airfield at Boyndie, four miles west of Banff, in April 1943. None of the blister hangars have yet been installed in this view from the south-west. Despite the obviously incomplete state, number 14 (Pilot) Advanced Flying Unit moved in during this month and began intensive flying training.

> **"IN FEAR AND TREMBLING"**
> B Flight groundcrew have discovered how to get 900 gallons of petrol into a 50 gallon tank. You just make sure there is no plug in the bottom of the tank.
> *Chocks Away, November 1944*

that gives the place such an inverted sense of real wartime glamour. This was an out-and-out combat airfield – an *action station* in every sense of the phrase. British wartime airfields like Banff were as different from peacetime RAF stations as it was possible to get. Before the war, new airfields were designed primarily to provide all the essential creature comforts for men and machines. Facilities for actually taking-off and landing the aircraft came well down the list of priorities. Aircraft hangars were huge permanent structures, grouped in threes around great concrete parking aprons (although concrete runways were not standard until war began). Mess halls for all ranks were big, spacious and well-equipped permanent brick buildings, often with a bit of design flair thrown in for good measure. Silver Service was the order of the day in the officers' messes. Even in the common-or-garden airmens' messes, dining rooms were huge, well-equipped, centrally heated and contained all manner of other facilities such as pubs, reading rooms and toilet and shower facilities. On the average pre-war RAF station therefore, life wasn't all that uncomfortable no matter what rank you were.

War – the great leveller – was about to quickly change all that.

The old cliché that Britain became one vast aircraft carrier during the Second World War is certainly true – but all those aircraft needed runways and airfield facilities. By the end of the war there were something in the order of 1,700 airfields scattered across the landscape of the British Isles. This represented an enormous programme of land acquisition and airfield construction, all of which would take time, resources, money and manpower. Something would have to give if they were all to be built, and that something was inevitably the creature comforts of pre-war RAF airfields. From 1940 onwards, the priority in airfield design became the needs of the aircraft, not the needs of the personnel. There could be no question of expensive permanent buildings. Gone were the extensive facilities and centrally-heated brick-built mess blocks. Now only a few key buildings would have

THE AIRFIELD

As good as it got: Nissen huts like this were the staple accommodation at Banff, and very few buildings were of permanent brick and concrete construction. This hut is the home to 333 Squadron's "B" Flight commander, and like most on the base it was treated to some tender loving care in the form of a small garden with white painted décor. Although all such huts were equipped with a simple stove, none were heat insulated in any way and in the depths of a Scottish winter could prove to be shockingly cold living quarters.

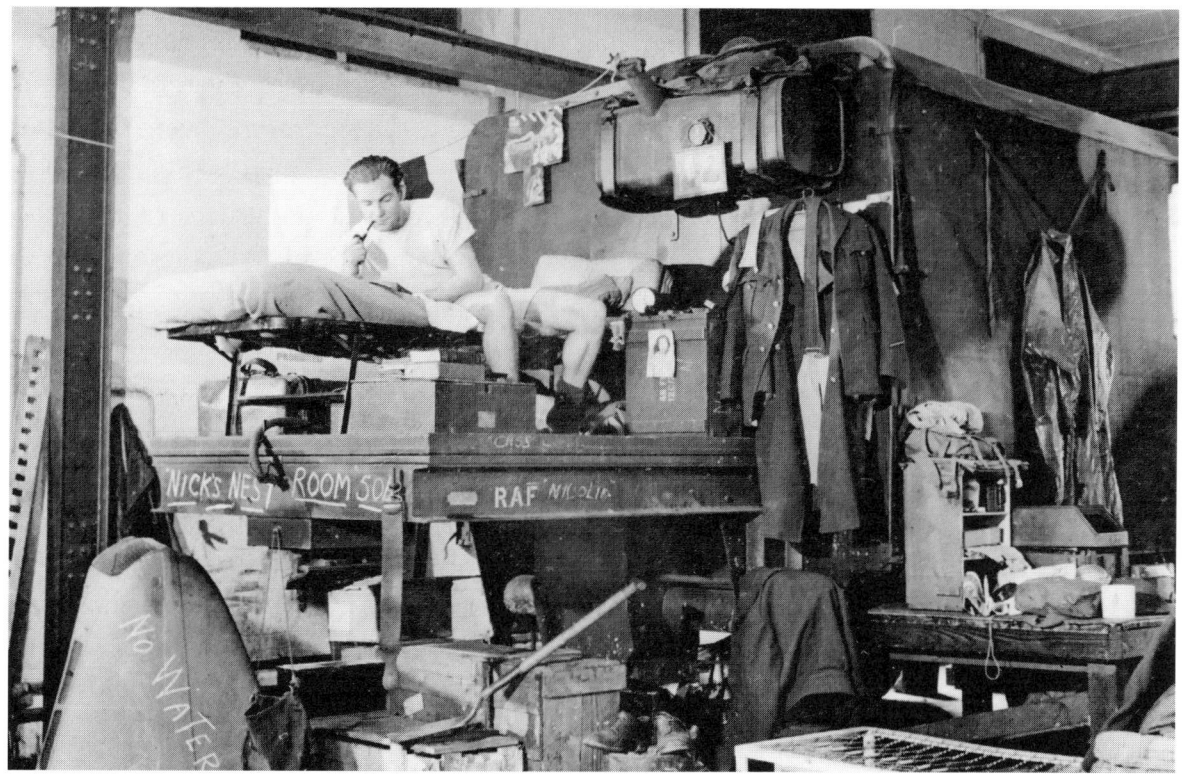

Any port in a storm. Due to the crowded accommodation at RAF Banff, Leading Aircraftman "Jock" Nicol took advantage of the relatively underused stand-by generator house and turned it into his personal billet. One of the few brick buildings on the airfield, with its distinctive flat concrete roof and steel beams, it stands there to this day deep inside woodland. Nicol has completed the makeover with a redundant truck chassis serving as a bed platform.

In the circuit at Banff: Taken from the south-west of the airfield by the navigator of a 235 Squadron Mosquito in 1945, this photograph shows how quickly the wounds of airfield construction have blended into the landscape. The neighbouring village of Whitehills is on the small headland immediately above the airfield. To the right of the picture, lie the fishing towns of Banff and Macduff, while beyond these is the distinctive headland of Troup Head.

Tony's animal magnetism: Although such a scene would be considered politically incorrect in the twenty-first century, WAAF's like these were effectively at the forefront of the feminist movement in their day, and they pushed the boundaries of equality by undertaking many previously male-dominated tasks on wartime airfields like Banff. Here, 144 Squadron Commander Tony Gadd takes donations for a Battle of Britain fundraising drive. Note also that in this supposedly more honest age, the donation box appears to be firmly padlocked.

THE AIRFIELD

brick or concrete lavished upon their construction. Everything else came second, but especially accommodation. These would have to make do with a type of building that has become synonymous with wartime airfields – the Nissen hut.

These tin sheds were distinctive because of their simple curved corrugated steel roofs, which allowed them to stand as monocoque structures with no need of rafters or roof trusses. They could be built quickly on a simple concrete base, heated by a stove with a chimney pipe straight through the steel roof – although this was usually where any heat went as well. Internal light was provided with a few bolt-on but draughty window frames. Each end could be in brick, tar-papered plywood or yet more corrugated steel. And Nissen huts were versatile. Any permutation of length and layout was possible. The main dining hall at Banff, for instance, comprised three one-hundred-and-fifty-foot long huts, joined by transverse huts providing access between them. The Sergeants and Officers messes were similar. Brick was often used to provide entrances, ante-rooms, kitchens or toilet blocks.

The blister hangar was, like the Nissen hut, an idea of simple genius. Using the same curved corrugated steel sheeting, small aircraft hangars could be built cheaply and quickly. Again, all they needed was a concrete base – a big one – and they were ready to use. Each end of these big steel arcs was left open, and a large canvas curtain provided to protect anything inside from particularly inclement weather. But although Nissen huts and blister hangars were relatively cheap and easy to build, when it came to inclement weather, there were few places like an airfield on a northern Scottish hillside in mid-winter to test out what they

Wide angle: A group shot of some ground crews and WAAF's with Max Aitken and other senior officers at Banff in the spring of 1945. This picture shows hangar number two on the technical site at the east of the airfield. These were type T-2 hangars, with the "T" standing for Transportable. All three on the airfield were auctioned off in 1946, with one being rebuilt ten miles away at Rosehall in Turriff, where it stood until the year 2001.

> **"IN FEAR AND TREMBLING"**
> An A Flight type had the NAAFI girls at the orange counter in tears over his wee bairn having no fun. They filled a large box with oranges and gave it to him. He was later seen behind a blister practically hidden behind orange peel and pips. What a conscience.
>
> *Chocks Away, April 1945*

were made of – a selection process that would also apply to the people forced to live in them.

When Coastal Command decided to build a new airfield in the parish of Boyndie near Banff in 1942, it must have seemed to those who ended-up being posted there that a certain amount of sadism had gone into the choice of location. It certainly seemed an unusual place to construct an airfield. The location was a ridge some 275 feet above sea level, just south of the rocky shore between the villages of Whitehills and Portsoy on the Moray Firth coast. The main east-west runway (runway number three) had a 25 foot height difference between the middle and the western end, while the rest of the airfield lay on slightly sloping land to the south. But it was clearly good enough for Coastal Command and, to be fair, there were airfields being thrown up in far worse locations. It was perhaps this veritable stampede for airfield construction sites all over the UK that led the RAF to take what they could get and grab the land at Boyndie. With German occupied Norway just across the North Sea (Banff is closer to Stavanger than it is to London), Coastal Command recognised quite early in the war that it would require airfields in north-east Scotland, even though they often (as in the case of Banff) had no initial idea what they would use them for. The general idea with the proposed airfield near Banff, was to make it suitable for a couple of squadrons of heavy bomber-type aircraft for long-range reconnaissance duties.

With this brief, the airfield construction work began at Boyndie in early 1942, and as it turned out, was a task that would leave a lasting effect on the nearby town of Banff itself. Aggregates were the first priority. Stones for the miles of deep concrete runways, perimeter tracks and access roads, as well as bases for several hundred huts and barracks were needed, and in enormous quantities. Quarrying for them locally does not seem to have been an option that was seriously considered, even though the nearby Durn Hill was already scarred by such a quarry. Instead, the

THE AIRFIELD

Slide rules and protractors: Navigators plan their routes the old-fashioned way at a briefing in the main ops room in the Operations Block at Banff. From the David Frost collection, his navigator "Alf" Fuller, sits in the front row with his hands inside his pockets, having apparently completed his notes and calculations before anyone else.

estuary of the River Deveron at Palmer Cove was stripped of it's pebble barrier, the river changed its course, and Banff Harbour became permanently silted-up.

Nevertheless, by April 1943, the new airfield at Banff was nearing completion. The layout was a standard one, with three runways laid out in a basic "A" shape. A long perimeter track snaked around the edges of the airfield, connecting all three runways. Some forty circular hardstandings known as "frying pan" dispersals led off the peri-track all around the airfield and also into the technical site. Here, nine of the hardstandings became home to blister hangars. Three main hangars were also dispersed around the airfield, and these were simple steel structures known as T-2 Hangars, with the "T" standing for Transportable. Apart from row upon row of Nissen huts, brick-built ablutions and air-raid shelters dotted the main sites on the airfield. These air raid shelters were basically pairs of four foot high walls, designed to protect personnel from strafing and bomb blasts, although not from direct hits. The potential blast of another kind was dealt with by locating the bomb dump, with its intricate network of tracks and loading ramps well to the north-east of the airfield, shielded

Its all gone now: The temporary wartime nature of RAF Banff is all-too apparent in this photograph taken near the station flagpole. Behind is the main dining hall, which was simply a connected group of three large Nissen huts. To the right of the halls is the station ration store, while to the left is one of the many personnel air raid shelters dotted about this area. Only these shelters and the long concrete floors of the dining halls can be seen here now.

Christmas 1944: People really made an effort on a wartime airfield like Banff, and 1944 was clearly no exception. Here in the station's main dining halls, the traditional custom of the officers serving the men is being observed on the only Christmas of Banff Strike Wing's existence. There were over three thousand personnel at Banff, however, and all three wings of the dining hall had to be used on separate sittings. In these days of strict rationing the feast on offer was very considerable, as was the effort that obviously went into the decorations.

deep within Whyntie Wood. The few buildings that received the full brick and concrete treatment were key ones such as the central Operations Block, the Control Tower (variously referred to in wartime as either Flying Control or the Watch Office), and the big standy-by generator set house. There was still a lot of work to do on the airfield, especially in terms of getting all the barrack block Nissen huts completed, yet despite these being incomplete, the first residents of RAF Banff began to arrive during that April of 1943.

By then, Coastal Command had reached the rather incredible decision that they no longer needed the airfield at Banff that they had just built, and passed it on to willing takers in the form of Training Command. Number 14 (Pilot) Advanced Flying Unit soon began arriving with their fleet of twin-engined Airspeed Oxford aircraft and settled into an intense period of flying training under their new station commander, Group Captain Peck. Many locals remember the high-pitched whine of the Cheetah engines of these small planes, with some clearly recalling that although the Oxfords were prone to crashing regularly around the airfield and its environs, they never seemed to catch fire when they did. The output of the training schedule was quite astonishing. In a little over a year at Banff, 14 (P) AFU turned out over 2,000 pilots, and undertook some 150,000 flying hours.

The new airfield attracted more than just trainees, however. William Bowling-Scott was an instructor with 14 (P) AFU at Banff, and claimed there were "so many strange things happening at Banff, which are best left unsaid". Rather enigmatically, he adds, "and I will never divulge them,"

> **"CHRISTMAS PROGRAMME"**
> Saturday, 23rd.   Officers Mess Dance.
> Sunday, 24th.   Airmen's Dance in Concert Hall.
> Monday, 25th.   Christmas Dinner – All Ranks Dance.
> Tuesday, 26th.   Sergeants Mess Staff Party.
> Wednesday, 27th.   Staff Dance.
> Thursday, 28th.   Sergeants Mess Dance in Concert Hall.
> Friday, 29th.   Recovery and Convalescence.
> Saturday, 30th.   Sergeants Mess – Invitation to WAAF & Corporals Mess.
> Sunday, 31st.   New Year's Eve Dance, all ranks.
> *Chocks Away, Xmas Edition, December 1944*

Christmas 1944: In another wing of the dining hall, and perhaps at another sitting, airmen and NCOs bring wives and local girlfriends along to enjoy the feast. The printed menu cards were a popular keepsake, and Max Aitken's signature appears on the back of the many examples of these menus that have survived. Among the officers in attendance here are the American Frederick Alexandre in the centre at the back, and the 248 Squadron Commander H.H.K. Gunnis, who has realised too late that he has just walked into the shot.

The show must go on: The harsh winter of 1944/45 was not allowed to interrupt strike operations, and snowblowers and ploughs were used to keep runways open. High-banked snow at the runway edges at Banff caused the crash of a Mustang fighter on take-off. The poor state of the thin layer of tarmac that was applied over the concrete is all too evident here, and hard frosts had soon broken up this surface before the airfield was even a year old.

THE AIRFIELD

A sea view: The decidedly coastal location of RAF Banff is evident from this shot of Max Aitken's Mosquito running-up on the northern perimeter track in 1945, one of the few level parts of the airfield. The majority of the station was built on a sloping elevated ridge – in other words, a hillside – and must have seemed to many to be an unusual location for an airfield.

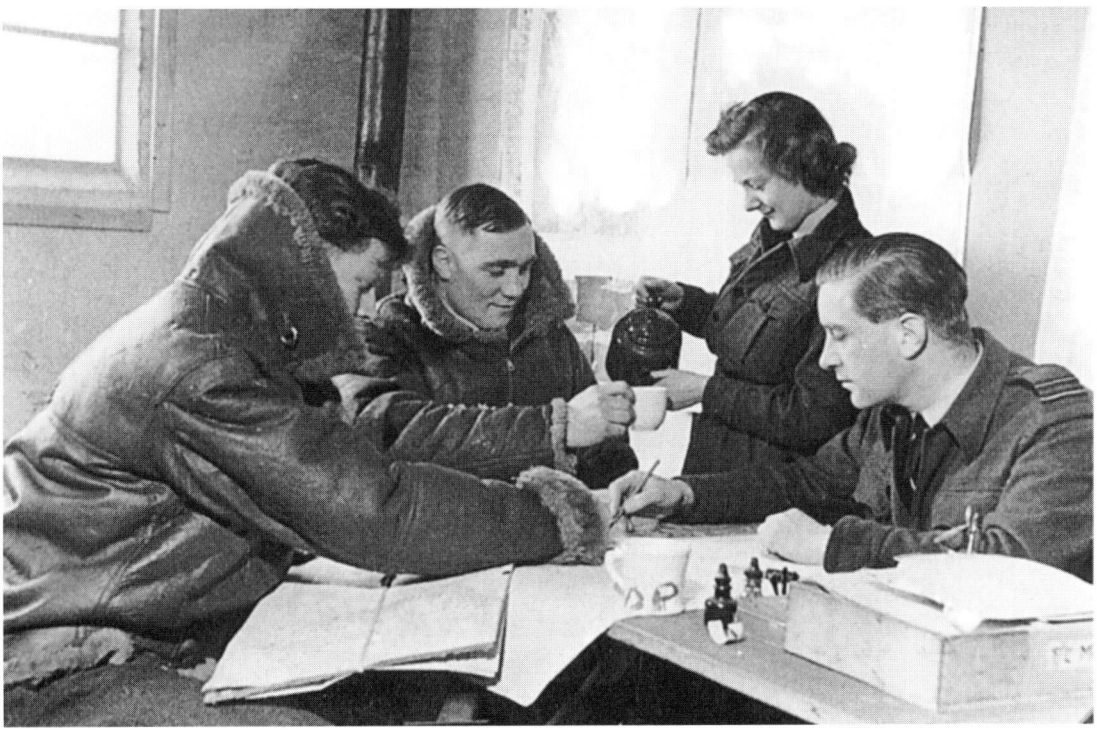

A brew before battle: WAAF Joyce Sherlock pours tea for a Mosquito crew in the Flight Offices at Banff as they go over last minute details before departure. The thick sheepskin flying jackets have become something of a humorous cliché today, but in the cold, draughty, unpressurised cockpit of a Mosquito, such basic protection was absolutely essential.

Crammed to capacity: A view of the western dispersals at RAF Banff in 1945. On closer inspection, no less than 48 Mosquitos can be seen parked around the "frying pan" hardstandings nearest the camera. The end of number one runway at the top of the picture became a permanent aircraft park, in order to ease the overcrowding caused by so many warplanes.

although he does claim that Banff at that time was used as a clearing post for agents and such like, coming from Nordic countries. Aircraft with civilian markings would indeed arrive and depart without explanation, yet had armed guards placed around them when parked on the airfield. Civilian Lockheed Lodestars were regular visitors, and one Imperial Airways example even arrived with an engine on fire. Even as it landed, a variety of "shady looking characters – both men and women", were seen to spill out of it all along the grass verge of the runway. For some reason, a group of Americans were also based here at this time. Nobody asked why. They kept themselves to themselves, shot craps all day and fattened-up their tame goose ready for the pot at Thanksgiving. In wartime, it was never wise to ask too many questions.

Neither did anyone ask any questions when, in July 1944, Coastal Command changed their minds and informed Training Command that they wanted their airfield back – and quickly. At the end of August, 14 (P) AFU was disbanded and scores of warplanes began to arrive in their place. The Beaufighters of 144 and 404 Squadrons came first, before being moved on a month

THE AIRFIELD

235 Squadron: The squadron's popular magazine was produced at Banff in this redundant bus, shown in a picture that virtually captions itself. The bus has been painted in the same mottled sea-grey camouflage scheme that all the Mosquitos based at Banff eventually wore.

VE-Day Parade: The predominance of the cheap and easily-built Nissen hut at Banff is clearly evident from this picture of personnel assembling for a VE-Day parade on the airfield in May 1945. The location of the scene is the recreation field behind the Airmens' Institute, while the huts in the background are the luxurious premises of the Officers' and Sergeants' Messes.

Pressing the flesh: On an open day at the sports fields at RAF Banff, Air Vice Marshal Simpson and a senior WAAF officer mingle with the crowds. Behind the WAAF officer, what would appear to be the local "spiv" seems to have turned up with his striped blazer and cravat.

No Squadron at all: Max Aitken performs a "fighter" style take-off in his personal Mosquito on a beautiful February day in 1945. Being station commander, Aitken was not a member of any squadron, and had to be repeatedly ordered not to fly on operations. It is not recorded how many times Aitken ignored this order, but it is known that he flew with the wing on the 8 May on a mission to Aalborg. This meant that he had flown operationally on the very first day, as well as the very last day, of World War Two.

THE AIRFIELD

later (much to their annoyance) up the coast to Dallachy. The Mosquitos of 235, 248 and 333 Squadrons then took up permanent residence at Banff, joined later in October by yet more Mosquitos, this time from 143 Squadron.

As always, the supporting ground crews of all these squadrons were forced to take the long way to Banff by truck and train, the latter option requiring a change at Aberdeen and then again at nearby Macduff, since there was no direct connection to the airfield from the south. Arrivals by train then faced a long walk up the hill to the station. Some got lost on the way. Betty Robertson was a young girl living at Cairnton Farm on the airfield perimeter. She clearly remembers some young airmen arriving from England at the height of a blizzard, knocking at the farmhouse door literally in tears at their extreme discomfort. If they were in tears then, one can only imagine their feelings on spending their first night in an ice-cold Nissen hut on that windswept hill in the middle of a blizzard.

Yet there was warmth to be had at Banff as well, in the shape of the remarkable comradeship and stoicism of servicemen and women at war. The RAF had sent their very best Coastal Command crews to Banff, and it showed. Hugh Donachie was a young pilot with 248 squadron who thought he'd seen it all until he walked into the Officers Mess at Banff for the first time. His peers, he realised, were all highly experienced and decorated. 'I'd never seen so many gongs in one place in my life' he would later recall.

Eventually, as the arriving ground crews began to fill up the airfield, accommodation became such a problem that even a Nissen hut came to be seen as something of a perk. Tents, for most of the year at least, were out of the question at Banff, and personnel either used their imagination in finding unusual places on the airfield to bed down in, or found lodgings as near to the airfield as possible. Officers could take advantage of more comfortable accommodation at places such as the Seafield Hotel in Cullen and the Commercial Hotel in Turriff.

Nearer the airfield, good pubs and watering holes were quickly identified, with the Shore Inn at Portsoy and the Fife Arms and

The main hub: WAAF officers inside the station offices, which were located inside the main brick-built operations block. This room and the building itself now lie empty but otherwise, as they were in 1945, still adorned with painted notices on the walls. Typical of the era, both WAAF officers have felt the need to be seen holding a cigarette for this publicity shot.

BANFF STRIKE WING AT WAR

Plough Hotel in Macduff being popular local venues. Naturally, high spirits led to high jinks, especially in Banff. The old cannon in High Street saw many failed attempts by airmen to haul it away. Diplomacy from the civilian police was required (although not always forthcoming) in the face of so many young service personnel letting off steam. Max Aitken, resourceful as ever, soon made friends with the local Chief Constable, George Strath, and would often use his influence to have wayward offenders transferred into the 'custody' of the station guardroom from the police cells in Banff.

There were similar stories in a great swathe of towns and villages all over what is now northern Aberdeenshire, where the local population received something of a culture shock at the sudden invasion of these young service personnel – but especially the aircrew. The trainee pilots of 14 (P) AFU had been young, untried and socially unsure of themselves. By contrast, the Mosquito and Beaufighter crews that sallied forth into the local pubs and hotels may have been equally as young, but any resemblance ended there. These were combat-experienced crews, who flew operationally with people shooting back at them. They were forced to take the losses of friends killed in action with fake outward stoicism, and were absolutely determined to make the most of life before it happened to them too. But the men and

The sun did sometimes shine at Banff: Another scene of the open day at the sports field. A running track has been marked out, and spectators including service personnel and local guests await the next event. The relationship with locals in the Banffshire area was always very good.

THE AIRFIELD

The best way to see it: The former wartime airfield at Banff as seen from the cabin of a Cessna light aircraft in 1986, looking east towards the neighbouring towns of Banff and Macduff. This flyby was an opportunity for a photo-shoot by the author, but is something that is no longer (technically) possible thanks to the huge wind turbines now dotted all over the airfield.

women of Banff Strike Wing became very popular. There were far fewer operational airfields in Scotland than in the southern half of England, and fewer opportunities for the local people to meet the real thing – battle-hardened aircrew – no matter how rowdy they often became.

Another aspect vividly remembered by people all across northern Aberdeenshire was the awesome sight and sound of Banff Strike Wing in the air. With often as many as 50 or 60 Mosquitos forming-up over Banff, joined by perhaps 30 or 40 Beaufighters from Dallachy, this huge formation would roar over central Buchan, rattling window frames with their massed throbbing drone. At the rallying point of Rattray Head lighthouse between Peterhead and Fraserburgh, they would be joined by a dozen or more P-51 Mustang fighters from Peterhead, before setting course out across the North Sea. On their return, often scattered, they would celebrate survival by "beating up" towns, villages, pubs and even individual houses of friends and girlfriends at very low level. They were a highly visible and audible presence in north-east Scottish skies, making victory seem all the more inevitable to those who witnessed them.

Back on the airfield, the overcrowding soon extended to the aircraft as well. With so many combat aircraft – at one point totalling 138 Mosquitos – parking spaces were at a premium. There were simply not enough hardstandings for all of them. Eventually, the southern end of number one runway was taken out of service and turned into a big aircraft park. Overcrowding caused accidents as well. On one gruesome occasion, a Mosquito taxied across the main runway just as another Mosquito was taking off on it. The cockpit of the taxiing Mosquito was ripped off and the crew decapitated. On another occasion, a visiting Wellington bomber flipped over on to its back on the northern perimeter track and exploded. Another visiting aircraft, this time a Lancaster bomber from 617 Squadron (the *Dambusters*) during the operation to sink the German battleship *Tirpitz* at Tromso, dropped its massive 12,000 lb. *Tallboy* bomb on one of the frying pan dispersals below the control tower in November 1944, causing the closure of the airfield for 24 hours until it was defused.

That little accident was amusing. Most were not, and the regular drip-drip of accidents during the nine month tenure of the Strike Wing was considerable. Aircraft collided in the circuit or simply crashed near Portsoy, Banff and Macduff. Others crashed on the airfield, or crash-landed after limping back across the North Sea with battle damage and wounded crew aboard. Such death and injury were the nature of wartime airfields. People pretended to be hardened to them, but in truth they never were. Personal letters and recollections tell a tale of crashes and small tragedies that have haunted those who witnessed them ever since.

The end of a squadron and an airfield: An artefact from the David Frost collection, few words are needed to accompany this poignant personal keepsake from more than sixty years ago.

When the war finally ended in early May 1945, the joy of VE Day was celebrated with abandon at RAF Banff. Bonfires were lit with anything that would burn. Officers had their ties cut off by WAAF's armed with scissors and the station commander himself, Max Aitken, was thrown into a fire water pool with a big grin on his face. Then, with astonishing speed, the airfield was wound down. Within a couple of months, all the squadrons had either been disbanded or transferred away. Ground crews received their discharge papers and finally went home. By the late summer of 1945, Coastal Command had fulfilled their original promise - RAF Banff was closed and lay utterly empty. From then on, the old airfield would be known locally as Boyndie 'drome, and is still signposted as such.

Though outwardly neither glamorous nor illustrious, old Boyndie 'drome had served her purpose, and served it well.

CHAPTER 3
THE MEN

MORE THAN THREE THOUSAND personnel worked day and night to sustain roughly two hundred and fifty men in battle at RAF Banff. This isolated minority were the aircrew, and they tended to be the cream of the crop. By the time the wing was formed in September 1944, five years of war had provided the RAF with a vast pool of highly experienced operational aircrew. It was why young Hugh Donachie had been so mesmerised by the amount of medal ribbons he'd seen the first time he'd walked into the Officers' mess. All of them were brave individuals with a string of stirring war stories already behind them. Yet when it comes to the story of Banff Strike Wing, one man must stand head and shoulders even above all these other notable characters, because by then he was already a national legend.

Group Captain, The Honourable John William Maxwell Aitken, DSO, DFC was the Station Commander of RAF Banff during the nine months of the Strike Wing's wartime existence. Technically, this meant that he was not part of Banff Strike Wing, nor a member of any of the squadrons, nor required (or even allowed) to fly on strike operations. But Aitken was far too blue-blooded a warrior to take any notice of this latter fact. He regularly flew on combat operations, despite repeated telegrams from 18 Group Headquarters ordering him not to do so. On the very last day of the war, he made a point of joining the wing on a sweep to Aalborg. This earned Aitken the distinction of having flown operationally on the very first day, as well as the very last day, of the war in Europe.

Born in Montreal on 15 February 1910, Max Aitken was the son of Max Aitken Senior, who later became better known as the press baron Lord Beaverbrook. Following the traditional

Man of War: This famous photograph of Group Captain Max Aitken by Illustrated *photographer James Jarche sums up the man perfectly. Highly experienced, decorated and heir to a newspaper empire to boot, Aitken had it all. A genuine member of "The Few", Aitken habitually disdained RAF dress codes, and was rarely seen without a silk cravat around his neck and his top button undone. But although relaxed and popular, he was also tough.*

Father and son: A rare photograph of Max Aitken with his father, the legendary Lord Beaverbrook, which was staged for Life *magazine. In their own way, each man made a major contribution to the war effort, and in recognition of his father's unique place in history, Aitken renounced "The Beaver's" hereditary title upon his death, declaring that there would only ever be one Lord Beaverbrook in his lifetime.*

upper-class education path through Westminster and Pembroke College, Cambridge, the young playboy then entered civil aviation, flying across Europe and the USA, before returning to England to join his father's *Express* newspaper empire. Like so many of his privileged peers, Aitken joined the part-time Auxiliary Air Force with 601 Squadron in 1935, a squadron populated entirely by other wealthy young men, who named themselves "The Legion". By the summer of 1940, Max Aitken was flying Hurricane fighters out of Tangmere and been promoted to the rank of Squadron Leader. He had already shot down eight enemy aircraft and been awarded the DFC. He was a nationally-recognised figure, and not just because of his famous father, who had been appointed Minister of Aircraft Production by Winston Churchill. The press had dubbed the rich playboy Auxiliary Air Force pilots *Max Aitken's Air Force* and although the name stuck, it soon came to be seen as a badge of courage and integrity, rather than the slightly derogatory term it had been conceived as.

> **"IN FEAR AND TREMBLING"**
> Butch Jacques has a good excuse for tossing back his favourite 'Schnorties', having evidently learned the difference between a brake lever and a cannon trigger.
> *Chocks Away, November 1944*

THE MEN

The men who really made it all happen: An impromptu group photograph of 235 Squadron ground crews at Banff captures the essence of these men, who would work many long and hard hours out on the dispersals in all weather to keep their aircraft on "top line" This group was officially known as number 8235 Servicing Echelon, and was taken in March 1945.

235 Squadron: Immediately prior to moving north to Banff from Portreath in Cornwall, 235 Squadron converted from their trusty old Beaufighters to brand new Mosquito FBVI's. Here, Wing Commander McConnell leads his men in a farewell pose with their old aircraft. The workmanlike nature of wartime aircraft is evident from the dents on the Beaufighter's nose.

Auxiliaries like Max Aitken not only refused to hide behind their wealth and social connections, but were also determined to prove their worth in the thick of battle.

Max Aitken himself once famously described how he felt, when interviewed by the makers of the groundbreaking television documentary series *The World at War* in the early 1970s. Asked if he had felt any chivalry towards the German fighter pilots he had been up against in the summer of 1940, Aitken – clearly offended

THE MEN

Angus prangs: On 16 February, 1945, Flying Officer Angus McIntosh from Grantown-on-Spey, together with his navigator Flying Officer Thorogood, were ordered to carry out a reconnaissance of the Norwegian coast between Utsire and the Naze. Over Egersund Harbour, he reported sighting four merchant vessels before being hit by flak. With one engine out of action, and with no flaps or undercarriage available, he flew across 227 miles of sea to make a successful crash landing back at Banff, although his Mosquito broke its back on landing.

by the question – retorted: "Certainly not. I *hated* them – they were trying to enslave us!"

Such sentiments meant that Aitken would never be satisfied fighting the war from behind a desk. The only times he ever used his considerable political contacts was when he wanted to get back into the thick of the action. Transferred to a desk job at the end of the Battle of Britain, Aitken eventually got himself posted to the command of 68 Squadron, which was a Beaufighter night-fighter

55

Celebrating survival with a pint: 248 Squadron Mosquito pilot Angus McIntosh, fourth from left in the back row, in happier times at the Shore Inn pub at Portsoy after a "clean sweep" in a darts tournament. One of many popular local watering holes for RAF Banff personnel, the rapport between the servicemen and the local people can be clearly seen.

Bill Sise: One of the most skilled and capable of the wing leaders at RAF Banff, Wing Commander Gage Darwent Sise hailed from Dunedin, New Zealand. As if to emphasise the gentle nature of this great warrior, he had originally trained as an accountant before the war. He was highly respected by all who knew him at Banff, due to his deep concern for the welfare of his men. Among his many achievements at Banff was getting married to WAAF officer Mary Crear in January 1945. He returned to Banff in 1989 as guest of honour to unveil the new Banff Strike Wing memorial, and died in Melbourne, Australia in 2003 aged 86.

squadron at Coltishall, where he brought his score of enemy aircraft destroyed up to 14 and earned a DSO in the process. Many of the crews in his squadron were Czech refugee airmen, and in recognition of his leadership and bravery, the Czech government in exile awarded Aitken the Czech War Cross. Once again, Aitken used his influence to get another posting to where the action was, and joined his then AOC-in-C, Sholto Douglas, in the Middle East in February 1943. Now a Wing Commander, Aitken was nonetheless back behind a desk, hating it with a passion, until promoted to Group Captain and put in charge of 219 Group at Alexandria and the fighter defence of North Africa. By now, he was not supposed to fly on operations at all due to his high rank, but nonetheless continued to do so unofficially. On the 5 March, 1944, he "borrowed" a Beaufighter, set off for the Aegean and had his own private "Junkers Party" when he shot down two German Ju-52 transport aircraft and claimed two others as probables. By the summer of 1944, Aitken was back in Britain and his old boss, Sholto Douglas, was now head of Coastal Command. Inevitably, Aitken sought out Sholto Douglas, who instinctively knew that Aitken was the right man to take command of the new Strike Wing he intended to create at Banff.

By then, Max Aitken was not only one of the immortal Battle of Britain "Few", but also an experienced night-fighter pilot and an outstanding commander with a genuine and burning determination to hit back at the enemy at every opportunity. Naturally, Aitken demanded the same sort of determination from his men, and although he could be very harsh with those who failed to live up to his standards, he was nonetheless considered by all who met him at Banff to be a truly great commander. From his days as a pre-war Auxiliary, Aitken habitually ignored rigid RAF dress codes, much to the consternation of his superiors at 18 Group and was rarely seen without a silk cravat in place of a service-issue tie, or his trademark Saville Row tailored (and red silk-lined) battledress tunic. As well as his qualities as a pilot and a leader,

> **"FAREWELL"**
> Reluctantly, we say 'cheerio' to 'Puppy' Calder and Les Floyd. They've played their little part in history adding to the Squadron's honours. Now they are on their way to a well earned rest. We wish them luck. Wherever they go, may the Fountain of Bacchus never run dry.
> *Chocks Away, October 1944*

He didn't bend this one: Angus McIntosh once again strikes a pose for the camera in his Mosquito. Taken near the ranges at Tain, this photograph was taken following the end of hostilities in 1945, and was admired so much that it was used as a Xmas card by the RAF.

```
CONFIDENTIAL.            RECOMMENDATION FOR HONOURS AND AWARDS.

Surname:-   McIntosh.                        Christian Names;- Angus Alexander.

Rank:-      Flying Officer.   Number:- 146325.    Unit:- No. 248 Squadron.

Command and Group.        COASTAL COMMAND.        No. 18 Group.

Number of Operational Sorties carried out:-   56

Total Operational Flying Hours:-              216

Particulars of Meritorious service, for which recommendation is made, including dates.

                          SEE OVERLEAF

State what recognition is recommended:-    Distinguished Flying Cross-Immediate.

State appointment held or how employed:-   General Duties Branch (Pilot).

                                           H.H.K. Gunnis.
Signature of Commanding Officer _____  S/Ldr.

Date:-_____

Covering remarks by Station Commander.
     This Officer has an outstanding record and is one of the main stays of the Banff Wing.
His keeness and intense desire to engage the enemy is an inspiration to all other crews.
He attempts to get on every sortie, and can only be kept on the ground by direct orders.
     On 9th. April 1945, his very accurate and close quarter R.P. attack resulted in the
disintegration of a submarine in the Kattegat, and again on the 11th. April, despite two
enemy fighters on his tail, he pressed home an attack on shipping in Porsgrunn Harbour,
regardless of the opposition from in front and behind.
     Most strongly recommended for the immediate award of the Distinguished Flying Cross.

                                              MAX AITKEN.
                                              Group Captain, Commanding,
Date:-_____                            R.A.F.   Station,   Banff.

Remarks by A.O.C.




                                              Air Vice Marshal,
                                              Air Officer Commanding,
Date:-_____                            No.  18  Group, R.A.F.

Remarks by A.O.C. in C.
```

THE MEN

Egersund Harbour: It is perhaps unsurprising that Angus McIntosh was hit by flak over this small fishing town. Attacked on two occasions by heavy strikes, the otherwise idyllic little harbour was well defended by anti-aircraft guns. On this occasion on the 24 of March 1945, two large merchant vessels and the flakship shown under attack here, were sunk. The distinctive boat sheds at Egersund are visible on the right of the picture.

333 Squadron: Young Norwegian aircrew from "B" Flight relax in the sun at Banff near their dispersals on the northern end of the airfield. These aircrew were not strictly part of the Strike Wing, but acted as "outriders", providing reconnaissance and navigational assistance over Norway for the main wing. Nonetheless, their hatred of the German occupiers of their country meant they never shied away from a fight – in fact, quite the opposite.

Before the storm: A photograph from the album of D.B. "Jack" Frost, who is standing on the right, taken at Banff on the 19th of September 1944. His caption reads: Taken on the morning of our last trip in the inevitable "H" for Harry, with "Casanova" the great A.L.F. Fuller and myself. *Frost is taking modesty to a new level here by not mentioning what happened to him and his aircraft later that day - as the documents below clearly demonstrate.*

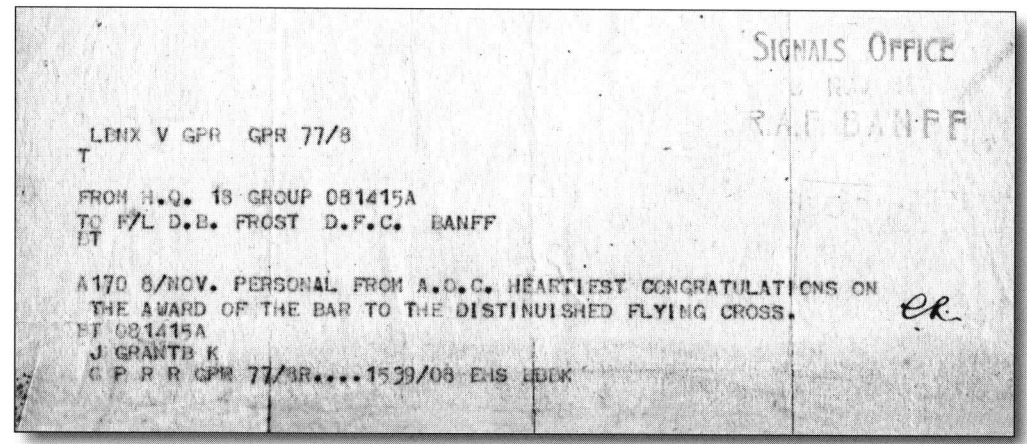

THE MEN

Gentlemen, this is where we will strike: Or so says the caption for this photograph in the Illustrated *magazine article of February 1945. On the left, Squadron Leader George Bellew looks on, while squadron commanders McHardy, Atkinson and Sise watch Max Aitken point out a few likely target locations on the map. Recently-married Bill Sise must have been off the flying roster, as he is in his best dress uniform instead of the battledress of the other pilots.*

 Copy.

CITATION

On 19th September 1944 in Mosquito H/235 in Wing Strike force of 12 Beaufighters armed R/P and 11 Mosquitos and 9 Beaufighters armed cannon and m/g, in anti-flak role, N. of Utuear, attacked 3 hostile M/V in face of opposition from all three and shore batteries north of STRONG FIORD.

In this very determined attack from 3,000 ft to 150 ft. F/O. Frost DFC., was wounded in the left hand, thigh and foot. In addition his port engine was put out of action. In spite of his injuries he succeeded in bringing his aircraft back to base on one engine and accomplished a successful landing and taxied to his dispersal point although on one engine, when he fainted.

He was taken to the Royal Infirmary, Aberdeen where his left little finger was amputated.

He has in my opinion shown great fortitude in this action which merits an immediate award of a Bar to the Distinguished Flying Cross.

COVERING REMARKS BY STATION COMMANDER.

This Officer has at all times shown great Gallantry and a keen desire to engage the enemy.

On his last sorties after a determined attack he brought his aircraft back to Base on one engine, although severely wounded.

Recommended for a Bar to Distinguished Flying Cross.

333 Squadron; Norwegian officers pose for a group shot on the balcony of the control tower at RAF Banff. Although actually a Royal Air Force squadron at this time, none of the officers wear RAF uniform, and instead sport a variety of Norwegian uniforms. Something of a law unto themselves, there were occasions when 333 Squadron aircraft returned to Banff hours after their fuel should have run out, and the Norwegians would form a human barrier around their aircraft to prevent non-Norwegian noses finding-out why. Max Aitken diplomatically ignored whatever it was they had been up to during these "missing hours" over Norway.

The Shore Inn, Portsoy: As the favourite watering hole of the young 248 Squadron Mosquito pilot Angus McIntosh, images taken in the public bar of this establishment naturally feature heavily in the personal photograph collection from his time with Banff Strike Wing.

THE MEN

Aitken's self-confidence was balanced-out by a charismatic and approachable personality, all topped-off by the sort of movie-star good looks that the press could never resist publishing whenever he posed for the camera in front of an aircraft propeller.

Despite his background, Aitken was no snob. Veteran 235 Squadron pilot "Puppy" Calder proudly claims that Aitken never looked down his nose at anyone – perhaps the ultimate compliment from a Canadian. Aitken was the type of commander who did not need to constantly prove he was the boss, and as a result commanded with a, *hail-fellow, well-met* type of authority that concealed the dedicated drive underneath.

Time after time, the veterans speak of their fond memories of him. WAAF Agnes Shaylor remembers her first meeting with her new boss at Banff. "This handsome man stepped out of an aeroplane and flashed us the most charming smile. We were so distracted that we simply never realised he was the new station commander." Other WAAF's recall his concern for his crews, and his obvious desire to keep everyone on the station informed. "He'd come on to the station tannoy whenever the wing returned," explained Joyce Sherlock, "and tell us that so many aircraft had been lost, and what they were doing to find any ditched crews".

When it came to looking after his people, Aitken had the effortless charm that allowed him to make friends easily and get whatever he needed to keep life on the station as happy as possible, be it tax-free whisky straight from local distilleries, or deals with landowners and farmers for meat and dairy produce normally never seen in the average wartime RAF mess. He commanded with the sort of Nelsonian blind-eye that his charges appreciated, because Aitken was always well aware of the deadly seriousness of the job that his people at Banff were involved in, but especially the aircrew who were doing all the fighting and dying. He was admired and respected, but particularly for his dogged determination to get on almost every mission the wing mounted. He never wanted to stop fighting. Many of the Banff veterans remember him not by the name of Max Aitken, but as *Bayhound Leader*, since the station control's call sign was *Bayhound*. Rarely was a station commander so honoured.

Given time, many of those who served under Aitken at Banff might well have achieved similar status. There was no shortage of contenders. All were battle-hardened and made of the same stuff as Aitken, although in so many different ways. Wing Commander

Flying Officer Harry Hollinson: Although a navigator with 235 Squadron, Hollinson exemplified the high "gong" rate of the aircrew at Banff by the DFC ribbon seen here on his tunic. In addition to fighting a war, Hollinson also somehow found the time to act as editor of 235 Squadron's monthly magazine.

Ready for action: Newly qualified, fresh-faced, and back in Britain after completing his flying training in Canada, David "Jack" Frost sports a battledress uniform as yet devoid of the many medals he would receive in the course of the war while flying Mosquitoes with 235 Squadron.

G.D. "Bill" Sise, for instance, was a shy, quiet-spoken former accountant from Dunedin, New Zealand. By the time he was 32, he was the commander of 248 Squadron at Banff, leading huge formations of Mosquitos into combat at low-level over Norway. Sise is particularly well remembered for his constant concern for the welfare of his men. Veterans recall how deeply and personally Sise took the losses of his men in combat. Yet still he carried on with steely determination. Sise balanced-out the violent nature of his job at Banff by getting married to Section Officer Mary Crear, a WAAF officer on the station, in January 1945. Although Bill Sise was only one of several squadron commanders who passed through Banff during those nine months, he was at least one of the lucky ones who survived. No less than four of the squadron commanders at Banff were killed in action while flying with the Strike Wing.

Among the rank and file aircrew of Banff Strike Wing, bravery and skill shone through equally as brightly. Flying Officer Angus McIntosh was a relative local, hailing from Grantown-on-Spey, and was only 22 years old when he joined Banff Strike Wing as a pilot in 1944. By the time he flew his last combat operation from Banff the following May, he'd had quite a few close shaves. On the 16 February, 1945, he and his navigator Bill Thorogood, were sent out on a solo reconnaissance of the Norwegian coast between

THE MEN

235 Squadron: Well and truly converted to Mosquitoes by the time this photograph was taken in March 1945, it shows the entire squadron including aircrew, groundcrew and WAAFs. The picture is from the collection of Alec Rix, who was a carpenter on the squadron's servicing echelon. Known as the Wooden Wonder, *the average Mosquito was glad of his skills*

Utsire lighthouse and the Naze. They ventured over the small harbour at Egersund, south of Stavanger, to take a look and were immediately engulfed in light flak. Their aircraft was badly damaged, with one engine out of action and the hydraulics destroyed as well, meaning they had no flaps or wheels for landing. In case they didn't make it, Angus sent out a report on the shipping he'd seen. They then had to decide whether to try to cross the vast North Sea on one engine, or to make a *Brighton Run*, meaning a landing in neutral Sweden where internment awaited, or to immediately crash-land in Norway, where even worse awaited. Both men agreed to try to get home, and arrived at Banff where they fired off a warning flare before coming in for a crash-landing. The Mosquito is an unforgiving aircraft to fly at the best of times, and Angus had to fight hard with his wounded machine

Flight Lieutenant Noel Russell: A typical Mosquito pilot with 235 Squadron was the painfully young looking "Russ" as he was known. Yet as always, this appearance was deceptive. Often leading a strike force himself, "Russ" was credited with shooting down two enemy fighters over Leirvik on the 11 January 1945, for which he was awarded a bar to his existing DFC.

> **"PRAISE"**
> Our expert single-engined-lander-of aircraft, Jack Frost, excelled himself recently when, wounded, he flew 300 miles on one motor and then made a wizard landing. We're rather proud of you Jack, and wish you a speedy recovery. His Navigator, Alfie, did a good job of first-aid, and fed his driver on barley sugar. Alfie however, was taking stronger nourishment when we saw him later that evening.
> *Chocks Away, October 1944*

489 Squadron: This New Zealand Squadron was based at Dallachy with Beaufighters. They moved to Banff in June 1945 to convert to Mosquitos, but found themselves being disbanded soon afterwards. Here, aircrew enact a scene for the post-war RAF documentary, The Shipbusters, *which focused entirely on the operations of the Banff and Dallachy wings.*

THE MEN

as it headed straight for the control tower, where the watching spectators on the balcony decided to jump to safety. Somehow, Angus managed to avoid the tower and put his aircraft down on the grass beside the frying pan dispersals, where both propeller assemblies were ripped-off and the aircraft broke her plywood back.

Max Aitken, as always, was unstinting in his generosity, declaring the crash to be the best belly-landing he'd ever seen. Angus and his navigator forced themselves back into another Mosquito the following day and flew a sightseeing sortie around Banffshire for "medicinal purposes". Soon, they were back on combat operations. Less than two months later, Angus took part in the sinking of three U-boats in the Kattegat. He was single-handedly credited with sinking one of the U-boats, which was seen to blow up after he had hit it with a full broadside from his rockets. He has always denied this accolade however, possibly because a film unit Mosquito following him in was caught and destroyed in the blast. Two days later, he was being shot at by a couple of enemy fighters while attacking shipping in Porsgrunn Harbour. Despite their hostile intentions, Angus continued his attack, fired his rockets, and only then turned to deal with his attackers. Back at base, his commanding officer, H.H.K. Gunnis, recommended Angus for a DFC, which Aitken immediately endorsed. To hear Angus speak of these events more than sixty years later (but only when prompted to) is to get the impression that it had all been a jolly good laugh and that the medals he had received, must surely all have been down to some sort of dreadful administrative error.

This sense of determined modesty is such a feature of the wartime generation, and is in stark contrast to the modern world in which the opposite seems to be the case. There were so many men just like Angus McIntosh in Banff Strike Wing, and it would be impossible to describe them all here, because they could all tell similar stories. For an outstanding example of this kind of self-deprecating modesty however, one need look no further than the personal wartime photograph album of Flight Lieutenant David "Jack" Frost, a pilot with 235 Squadron. In one page of his album is a solitary photograph of Frost and his navigator posing in front of their Mosquito. Frost has written merely the date of the picture – 19 September 1944 – followed by the enigmatic caption:

And not forgetting the women: Young WAAF Agnes Shaylor found anonymous national fame with this photograph of her with a 25lb solid-shot rocket projectile over her shoulder, which appeared in the 1945 Illustrated *article on Banff Strike Wing.*

Wing Commander A.K. "Ken" Gatward: Commanding officer of the Canadian 404 "Buffalo" Squadron, Gatward poses in the "office" of his Beaufighter. Initially based at Banff, the Buffaloes were transferred to Dallachy, then eventually back to Banff again for conversion to Mosquitoes – just in time for the war to come to an end.

Bent but not broken: A 235 Squadron Mosquito lies on the grass at Banff after a successful belly landing by it's pilot, Flight Lieutenant Shields. Known by the slightly cruel nickname of "Killer" by his squadron crewmates, Shields earned the name soon after his first combat, when he openly admitted to a certain amount of angst at having killed a man for the first time.

333 Squadron: From the collection of Ole Inge Lindaas, both he and several of his fellow "B" Flight veterans insist on the same story behind this photograph. The legend has it that this Norwegian Mosquito was recalled to Banff with the words, "the war is over, come back" and that a celebratory group picture was taken in front of it when it returned to Banff.

THE MEN

Taken on the morning of our last trip in the inevitable "H" for Harry, with "Casanova", the great A.L.F. Fuller and myself.

What Frost fails to mention is *why* this was their last trip in "H for Harry". During an attack on a convoy in the otherwise idyllic Norwegian fjord at Askevold, Frost and his aircraft were hit by a 37mm flak shell which exploded in the cockpit. Badly injured in the left hand, thigh and foot, and bleeding alarmingly, Frost was also faced with the loss of one engine as well. He would have been well-advised to land there and then in Norway, where medical attention was at least guaranteed, even if it would also mean spending the remainder of the war in captivity. Instead, Frost took the great risk of crossing the North Sea, in the hope that both his remaining engine and his own blood supply would hold out until he got home. Back at Banff, he not only landed successfully, but also carefully taxied his aircraft back to its allotted hardstanding, where he finally allowed himself to faint from lack of blood.

It took longer to drive Frost the fifty miles into Aberdeen Royal Infirmary than it had for him to fly back from Norway, but once there his left little finger was amputated. Within a month, Frost was back in action at Banff, having taken advantage of his sick leave to get married. Max Aitken had recommended an immediate bar to Frost's existing DFC medal, and back in his native town of Maldon in Essex, the local newspaper celebrated his award with an article headlined with the words; *Maldon's Bonnie Fechter*, in reference to the fact that Frost, like so many of his fellow Mosquito pilots, were doing their *fechting* from northern Scotland.

These men seem like truly exceptional individuals to those of us who have never been faced with such terrible circumstances. And yet in terms of Banff Strike Wing, these same men would never have considered themselves to be exceptional in any way. As far as they were concerned, everyone else was doing the same job. But what *does* make all of the men mentioned here exceptional, is that they survived the experience.

Eighty-five other men from Banff Strike Wing, were not so lucky.

CHAPTER 4
THE MACHINES

THE TASK OF FINDING, attacking and sinking a ship in the average warplane of 1945, required considerably more skill and courage than needed to do the same job using the technology of a twenty-first century warplane. The difference is so pronounced that it is worth comparing them, in order to illustrate just how difficult and dangerous it was to operate the machinery of war employed by Banff Strike Wing.

The Wooden Wonder: The De Havilland Mosquito was developed as a speculative venture without the benefit of an Air Ministry specification. Built basically of laminated plywood in order to save precious aluminium, the aircraft proved to be fast, tough and extremely versatile. It served as both a fighter and a bomber, was faster than early Spitfires, and could carry an enormous payload. Adapted for use with Coastal Command, it became a potent ship-killer.

Today, with unmanned drones like the MQ-1 Predator with its *Hellfire* missiles, even pilots are no longer always a requirement. When they are, the average F-18 Hornet pilot still has a far easier and safer life than that of a wartime Mosquito crew. An F-18 strike fighter pilot is now more of a systems operator than airman, strapped into a software-controlled data-processing machine that will take him (extremely quickly) to within a few feet of any precise spot on the planet he wants to go, then take him all the way home again, day or night, whatever the weather. When the pilot wants to undertake something as simple as attacking a ship, his systems can not only locate it for him at a great distance but also automatically target it for him as well. On the press of a button,

THE MACHINES

281 Squadron: The crews of the Vickers Warwick aircraft based at Banff were a detached flight of their main squadron, which had similar detachments on coastal airfields all over the UK. The air-dropped lifeboat can be clearly seen under the belly, although not quite so obvious, is the pile of still-wet seaweed that some wag has placed above the small air intake under the starboard engine for this staged photo-shoot.

Whispering Death: The nickname given to the Bristol Beaufighter was due to it's relatively quiet Hercules radial engines, which could still run with entire cylinders shot away. Tough and versatile, the magnificent Beaufighter was only bettered by the Mosquito. This rocket-equipped example demonstrates the aircraft's low-flying prowess as well.

A sight worth seeing: The eighteen-ship formation seen earlier has now passed right over the control tower in this dusk photo shoot in October 1944. This formation, like all Strike Wing formations, consisted of a mixture of aircraft from all the squadrons then based at Banff.

The office: Giving some idea of the cramped confines inside the cockpit of a Beaufighter, this photograph shows how the pilot's gunsight could be swung out of the way for better visibility.

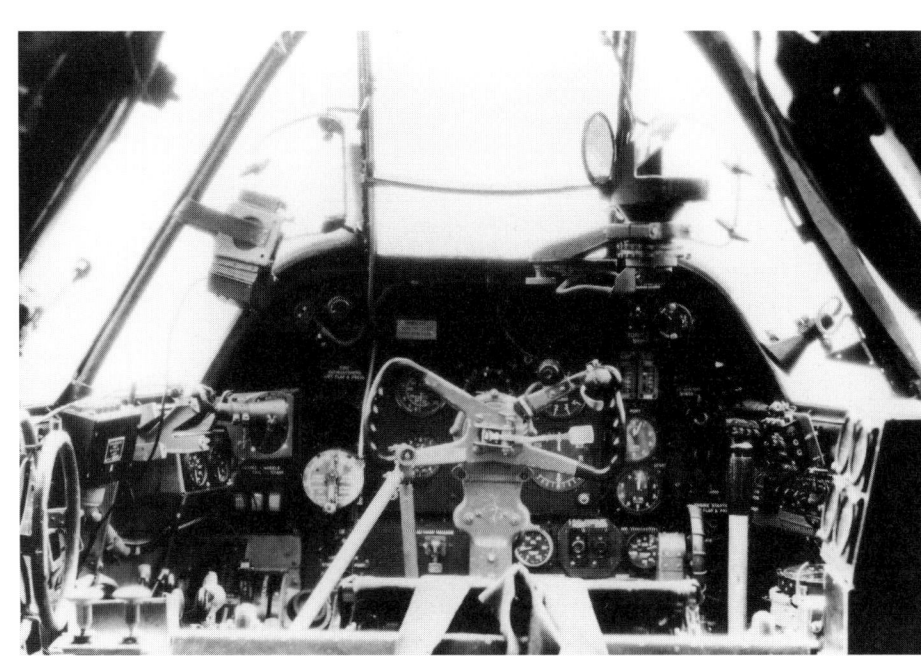

THE MACHINES

Caught at sea: This photograph of 144 Squadron Beaufighters attacking shipping shows how dangerous the open sea was for merchantmen venturing out during the day. Debris flies out from the target as a Beaufighter banks almost vertically away. Meantime, the aircraft taking the photograph is flying lower than the tops of the ship's masts.

the systems will launch his AGM-84 *Harpoon* anti-shipping missile for him up to 50 miles away from the target, then allow the pilot to forget all about it as he turns for home. Meanwhile, the missile will have dropped to sea-level and be skimming along at 500mph, using its radar and computer to keep an eye on the target. Even when the missile gets there, if it is not too happy with the approach, it will go around and try again, before impacting itself on the unlucky ship.

Meanwhile, aboard his flying real-time video console, if the F-18 Hornet pilot runs into trouble and has to abandon his aircraft in an emergency over the sea, he is still in a far better position to

"CLUELESS CROSS"

The Ancient Moronic Society of Clueless Clots this month awards the Clueless Cross to Corporal . . . . and L.A.C. . . . . for conspicuously furthering the war effort. In the gathering dusk of a recent evening, aircraft were being refuelled and the corporal whose technical knowledge is not his strong point, decided to assist the LAC by filling the "belly" tank of one of the aircraft. After emptying the contents of one Bowser into the tank, the corporal became suspicious and investigated the apparently large capacity of the tank, through the open bomb doors. There, he discovered two medium sized bombs where the tank should have been. His next action almost lost him this coveted award. In silence he erected a sign on which was inscribed the words, "NO SMOKING".

Chocks Away, November 1944

Torbeau: The first Beaufighters of numbers 144 and 404 Squadrons to arrive at Banff, were equipped for anti-shipping operations with a single underslung torpedo. Increasingly, the nature of close-quarter attacks inside Norwegian fjords led to rocket-only armaments.

248 Squadron: Something of a self-portrait from the personal collection of Group Captain Angus McIntosh, RAF (retired). Here, a 248 Squadron aircraft flown by Angus shows the distinctive black spinners with white tips that many of the squadron's aircraft wore. Also visible are the guard rails between the rockets and drop tanks.

THE MACHINES

do so than his ancestors in their old propeller-driven Mosquito. Thanks to the technology of the ejector seat, he can exit the aircraft quickly and cleanly and be assured that he will land reasonably safely in the water, where satellite tracking beacons, transponders and all manner of other locating devices will immediately jump into life and begin electronically shouting out to the world – *He's here!* If a helicopter does not quickly race to his aid, the appearance of a ship homing-in on the spot is guaranteed almost anywhere on the modern world's oceans. Meanwhile, to keep him alive, a state-of-the-art immersion suit will prevent his body from trying to heat up a freezing ocean and keep hypothermia at bay until rescued.

By contrast, when finding themselves in similar sorts of trouble over the North Sea in 1945, the crew of a crippled Mosquito would know that they were almost certainly doomed. That is why the decision to head back out across the North Sea on one engine (which may stop running halfway across) was always such a brave one. If the crew had to get out of a Mosquito, they usually had to get it down out of the sky first, since the *Wooden Wonder*, for all its fame, was a notorious brute of a machine to try to get out of in a hurry. This simple task was made even harder if the aircraft was rapidly sinking into the freezing North Sea. The statistics stacking up against their survival then became even worse if they made it

Striped casualty. Another view of the belly-landed Mosquito of Flight Lieutenant Shields at Banff in the autumn of 1944. The aircraft still wears its post D-Day invasion stripes, although these began to be partially and then fully painted-out as the year 1944 drew to a close.

Who needs rockets: A Mosquito FBVI demonstrates the firepower of its fixed armament. Four browning 0.303 machine guns were fitted in the nose cone, while in the belly were four big 20mm Hispano cannon. These latter weapons were powerful enough to destroy a merchant ship entirely on their own. When used defensively against enemy fighters, this combination of cannon and machine guns could prove devastating.

Trial and error: This detail from a posed shoot for Illustrated *magazine at Banff in October 1944 shows rockets being loaded on to the early design of rocket rails. These rather complex rails often caused rockets to jam when fired, and a simpler rail design was quickly sought.*

THE MACHINES

out of the aircraft. If they had a dinghy, hypothermia might take an hour or so to kill them on an average day in the northern North Sea. If they did not, cold water immersion would definitely kill them within 15-30 minutes. No beacons would broadcast their position. No helicopters would come. Pure God-given luck was their only hope of survival.

Understandably, Coastal Command had to do something to reassure crews faced with such terrible prospects. At Strike Wing airfields, detached flights from number 281 Squadron were based with big twin-engined Vickers Warwick ASR (Air Sea Rescue) aircraft. These white-painted aircraft were equipped with either *Lindholme* survival equipment comprising liferafts and supplies, or with a single parachute-dropped fully-equipped lifeboat. Warwicks would follow the routes of strike missions and drop this equipment to ditched crews, then remain circling them to guide rescue ships to the scene – provided any were in the vicinity. After dark, the Warwicks would have to return to base and any survivors were once again on their own. But it was better than nothing. Although air-dropped lifeboats did not always deploy and sometimes broke-up on hitting the water, there were instances in which they did the job they had been designed for, and in the age before helicopters and transponder beacons, it was perhaps the best that Coastal Command could have provided.

But these were only the results of having to "ditch" in the North Sea. Mosquito and Beaufighter Strike Wing crews had lots of other equally cheery potential problems to occupy their thoughts all the way to the target and back. Usually, these simply involved getting their machines into the air and keeping them there, then finding their way to Norway. Not as easy as it sounds today. Strike Wing aircraft had evolved during the war from the Blenheims and Beauforts of the early years into the highly potent Beaufighters and Mosquitos. For their day, these aircraft were a vast improvement on their predecessors, but nonetheless, they were still hard work to fly, let alone fight in. It is not the intention here to list the technical specifications and capabilities of these aircraft, but simply to try to show what they were like as the tools of the trade for the Strike Wing crews who used them.

Despite being the more outwardly glamorous of the two, the de Havilland Mosquito FBVI was a relatively late arrival to the world of anti-shipping strikes, only appearing on the scene in late 1943. The Bristol Type 156 Beaufighter however, had become the

That's better: Designers soon came up with the simple one-piece aluminium rocket rail and the aircraft of both Banff and Dallachy Strike Wings were quickly refitted with these rails. Simple steel clamps held the rockets in place, and these slid along a groove either side of the rail both for fitting and launch. In this shot, the rockets are the 60lb explosive head type. In 1999, the author found a stack of these distinctive rocket rails in the yard of a Banffshire farm.

Pigtails: An armourer screws in the electrical firing wires for the rockets on a Beaufighter, known as pigtails. Not only does this picture show the early rocket rails, but also the early over-confidence of this armourer. So many rockets launched themselves prematurely as soon as they were connected, that it became normal practice to plug in the pigtails only when the aircraft was ready to roll. And for the armourer to stand well clear – just in case.

THE MACHINES

master of the art as soon as it entered service with Coastal Command in 1941. The first big Strike Wing was based at North Coates on the Lincolnshire coast, and the tactics employed were developed and refined here as lessons were learned. On shipping strikes before the Mosquito came along, a mixture of Beaufighters were used, some being armed with an 18 inch torpedo (known as Torbeaus) which had to be launched at very low level, and others purely with their four belly-mounted 20mm cannon and wing-mounted 0.303 inch machine guns in a flak-suppression role. By 1943, the anti-flak Beaufighters began to be armed with the first versions of wing-mounted rocket projectiles as well. These rockets were the forerunners of the kind of air-launched missiles that almost every future warplane would employ in combat.

But the rockets pioneered by Coastal Command were basic, and were in effect little more than fireworks in principle. Comprising a four foot long steel tube, three inches in diameter and with a set of four fins serving as a tail, they were filled with cordite propellant which was ignited by an electrical charge at the flick of a switch. Initially fitted with 60lb high explosive warheads, these first rockets could indeed sink ships, but needed a lot more of them to do it than those fitted with a simple 25lb solid shot warhead. These latter versions were found to have considerable armour-piercing capabilities, and with the ability to punch through steel up to four inches thick, were quickly recognised as a far more effective anti-shipping weapon. By late 1944, the eight rockets fitted underneath the wings of both Beaufighters and Mosquitos were almost exclusively of the solid shot type which, to the delight

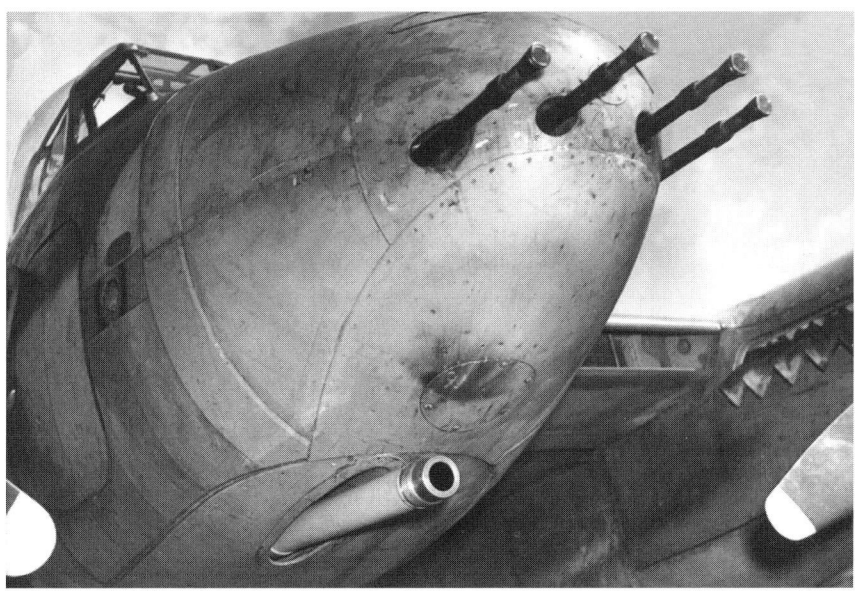

Protective measures. The considerable muzzle flash and blast of the 57mm anti-tank gun fitted to the Tsetse versions of the Mosquitos at Banff required extra protection for the airframe. Here, the strengthened panel under the nose of the aircraft can be clearly seen, as can the soot-blackened markings caused by the repeated firing of this fearsome gun.

of the crews who fired them, were found to be able to penetrate the pressure hulls of U-boats with ease. But the effect was quite a nasty one for those on the receiving end. Whether the target was a ship or a U-boat, once a solid-shot rocket had penetrated and entered the hull, the still-burning propellant would cause the projectile to thrash around inside, killing anyone near it. Meantime, the hole it had made would be causing the vessel to sink.

Rockets could be fired in pairs, or as an entire salvo of eight, which the RAF of the day liked to compare to the broadside of a cruiser, although this is perhaps rather an optimistic description. The weapon was reasonably accurate, although unlike a modern stand-off missile, had to be launched very close to the target, due to the fact that the cordite propellant was not the ideal fuel and therefore the range was not very long – only as much as a few hundred yards. Gravity also took a hand with these heavy projectiles, and rockets began to follow a ballistic downward curve almost as soon as they were launched. In many of the filmed and photographed scenes of rocket attacks by the Strike Wings, the rockets are seen to curve downwards and enter the water in front of a ship, but this was no miss – it was deliberate. It was found that the rockets, upon entering the water, refracted upwards and kept on running towards the ship, crucially punching their holes below the waterline. Aiming became quite a skill therefore, and the forward machine gun armament of both types of aircraft were used to "walk" the fire toward the target, so that pilots could gauge just the right point to release their rockets. By then, the heavier cannon fire would be unleashed as well, and these powerful 20mm shells could often be enough to sink the relatively thin-skinned merchant vessels on their own. Even when hit above the waterline, the superstructure of a merchant ship raked from

---

"IN FEAR AND TREMBLING"
A certain pilot left his VHF switch on the other day, and many people may have heard the following conversation:
Deep Brown Voice: "There's quite a wind today."
Sweet Female Voice: "Yes ... Isn't there."
Deep Brown Voice: "Not a very good landing, I'm afraid."
Sweet Female Voice: "Didn't say anything."
Deep Brown Voice: "Well, you have had your flip AFTER all."
Sweet Female Voice: "Thanks ever so."
Chocks Away, Xmas Edition, December 1944

THE MACHINES

Bent Beaufighter: This unidentified machine has successfully belly-landed at Banff. Such a landing was usually caused by hydraulic failures caused by combat damage, and since both propellers were clearly turning when the aircraft landed, this would seem to be the case here.

Ground Study: The Mosquitos of number 143 Squadron at Banff became the most intensely photographed examples of the breed anywhere in the world, when Max Aitken – who knew about such things – repeatedly put the squadron and its aircraft at the disposal of the press.

Servicing and refuelling: This Mosquito carries the distinctive red white and blue markings applied to the spinners of all the Norwegian 333 Squadron aircraft based at Banff as a morale-booster to their fellow countrymen. The picture was taken in May 1945 at Gardermoen airfield near Oslo, when the Norwegians finally went home, taking their Mosquitoes with them.

Feeding the beasts: An enormous amount of rockets were required to keep the Mosquitoes of Banff Strike Wing in action. In a typical scene before a strike, armourers load up a 143 Squadron Mosquito on the frying pan dispersals south of the control tower in February 1945.

THE MACHINES

end-to end by one aircraft after another, all letting fly with their 20mm cannon, inevitably required major repairs to the superstructure and deck fittings. And to the crew . . .

If that was bad enough for the ships on the receiving end, worse was soon to follow in the shape of the rather remarkable Mk XVIII "Tsetse" Mosquito. This was an aircraft unique to Coastal Command, and involved stripping-out the four belly cannons and replacing them with a single 57mm quick-firing Molins anti-tank gun. The six pound shells fired by the Tsetses were enough to sink a ship or a U-boat entirely on their own. The massive gun had a wicked recoil however, and crews could actually feel the aircraft slow down suddenly each time the gun was fired. Although impressive, the Tsetse – so named for its more lethal sting – was not used in large numbers, and only a few examples flew with 248 Squadron at Banff.

Rockets – the staple weapon of Banff Strike Wing – had the potential to be equally as lethal to the ground crews who fitted them as they had to enemy ships. The electrical connections to fire the rockets were known as "pigtails" and after a few instances of rockets self-launching when the pigtails were connected on the ground by armourers, self-preservation came to the fore, and pigtails were then only connected (very carefully) when the aircraft were running and ready for take-off. A full load of eight rockets used-up all the underwing hardpoints on a Mosquito however, meaning long range fuel drop tanks could not be carried as well, something that was essential for operations over Norway. The problem was solved with simplified launching rails (the early

Welcome to Scotland: It seems inconceivable that aircrew would be ordered to take off in such terrible weather, let alone fly across the North Sea, fight a determined enemy, then somehow try to find their way back to base in these atrocious conditions. But they did, as this wintry scene at Banff demonstrates. This is the same area as the "taxi rank" photograph.

A precarious job: Sweeping snow off the wings of aircraft became something of a photogenic if common activity in the winter of 1944/45. This 235 Squadron Mosquito receives the treatment from a nervous-looking airman before another sortie out over the hostile North Sea.

ones often caused rockets to jam) stacked one above the other, allowing the big paper-mache drop tanks to be fitted as well. The first time they were tried out, it was found that when the empty drop tanks were jettisoned, they sometimes fouled the rocket rail assemblies as they fell away, so a guard rail was fitted to prevent this.

Armed with rockets, cannons and machine guns, filled to the gunwales with fuel in onboard tanks and in external drop tanks, and laden down with as much ammunition as it could carry, the average Beaufighter or Mosquito then had to get into the air. With none of the enormous jet thrust of a modern day strike aircraft, this was no easy matter. Wartime aircraft were routinely overloaded beyond their peacetime limits, and take-offs were always hard work. In piston engined tail-dragger aircraft like these, too much sudden power could cause the machine to pitch forward on to its nose, destroying the propellers and shock-loading the airframes. Power had therefore to be applied gently on take off, and yet as soon as the tail came up, the torque effect from the engines would drag the aircraft off to one side, requiring a well-timed boot-full of opposite rudder from the pilot until the aircraft came unstuck. If an engine failed at that crucial moment, the aircraft would fall back down again. With so much fuel and ordnance aboard, this was not an attractive proposition. Once

> **"GET A LOAD OF THIS"**
> Which is coming to which and why, when a sergeant walks into his office and says; "What's all this I hear about a serviceable aircraft?" And by the way, we hope LAC Rees collected his police summons from the orderly room.
> *Chocks Away, Victory Edition, May 1945*

THE MACHINES

Our tailwheels didn't always work on ops: So runs the caption to this photograph from David Frost's photo album. As long as the tailwheel was stuck in the down position rather than up, a small technical fault like this would not stop operational crews from "pressing on" as the phrase had it. Taken by Frost's navigator on a sortie across the North Sea, it shows a 235 Squadron machine in close formation with a 248 Squadron aircraft in the autumn of 1944.

Peterhead Mustangs: A rare shot of a formation of P-51 Mustang fighters of number 19 Squadron, who moved north to RAF Peterhead on 14 February 1945 and remained there until the end of the war, providing long-range fighter escort to the Strike Wings over Norway. Already blessed with long range, they also carried additional fuel in underwing drop tanks.

85

formed-up over Banff, the journey to Norway had to be undertaken. There was no radar or other complex navigation aids carried on Strike Wing aircraft, and courses had to be navigated the old-fashioned way on maps using protractors and rulers, calculating wind-speed, airspeed, drift and other factors manually and mentally en-route. Norway has an enormous coastline, and the fact that the Strike Wings managed to find their way to precise target locations time after time is testament to an art of seat-of-the-pants aircraft navigation that is all but extinct today.

Then there was the flight itself to contend with. Mosquitos and Beaufighters were weapons of war. Unpressurised, they were not only cold, but draughts blew in from all manner of semi-sealed orifices in a machine doing several hundred miles an hour. The sheepskin flying clothing, no matter how much mocked and derided today, was utterly essential for anyone flying in a wartime aircraft. The Strike Wings flew very low, which caused its own problems. Approaching an enemy coast under the radar was important in order to try to achieve some surprise, and Strike Wing veterans habitually claim that they flew all the way to Norway and back at fifty feet. This may not be an entirely reliable fact, yet even if another hundred or so feet were to be added to this height estimate, the flight would still be a very uncomfortable and dangerous one. At such low levels, high speed flight over the sea makes for an extremely bumpy ride. Added to this is the fact that if a technical problem were to suddenly arise and the aircraft lost height, or even if the pilot lost concentration for a moment, it would take only a couple of seconds for the aircraft to hit the water at high speed, killing everyone aboard. After a mission they'd have to do it all over again on the way home.

If all this wasn't bad enough, people would then start shooting at them as well. The various types of flak that could be employed

Flying artillery: Several of the 248 Squadron aircraft at Banff were the heavily modified Mark XVIII "Tsetse" Mosquitos (because of the more powerful "sting"). These had their four cannons removed, and in the case of this aircraft, two of its machine guns as well. In their place went no less than a big six-pounder, 57mm calibre Molins quick-firing anti-tank gun.

THE MACHINES

by the German defenders against Strike Wing aircraft have already been discussed, though not the effects they could have. Light flak had to score a hit to cause any damage, since it exploded only on contact. Larger calibre flak, right up to the dreaded 88mm type, were fused to explode in mid-air. They were designed to shower splinters of white-hot metal shell casings all over the sky. Sometimes a splinter would hit a fuel tank and blow a wing off, or perhaps enter the cockpit and rip a pilot's head off. Flak was highly unpleasant stuff to face. Most of the time, flak simply caused puncture wounds in either the aircraft or its crew. Like David "Jack" Frost over Askevold in September 1944, it was all a matter of luck whether the injuries caused a pilot to bleed to death before he got home or not. Flak hitting an aircraft and causing damage however, always had a far more profound effect on a Mosquito than it did on a Beaufighter.

The reason for this was very simple. Mosquitos were fitted with liquid-cooled Merlin engines, whereas Beaufighters had Hercules radial motors. In combat conditions, a pilot would always prefer a radial engine over a liquid-cooled one if he had the choice. Even a small flak splinter puncturing a radiator or a coolant line in a Mosquito would quickly cause the Merlin engine to overheat and shut down. Radial engines such as those fitted to Beaufighters by contrast, were air-cooled and needed no liquid. Their independent cylinder arrays could keep running even with entire cylinders shot away. A counterbalance to all this was the plywood construction of the Mosquito, which proved to be extremely combat resilient in comparison with standard aluminium airframes. They could withstand considerable damage and still stay in one piece. Following a mid-air collision over Banff in early 1945, Wing Commander Gunnis from 248 Squadron even landed with half his starboard wing missing. The crew of the other aircraft were not so lucky. In an unforgiving wartime flying machine with no ejector seats, they were unable to escape in time before the ground rushed-up to meet them.

Unlike modern-day jet jockeys, Strike Wing aircrew faced almost as much danger from the machines and the elements they flew in, as they did from enemy guns.

It is easy to get nostalgic about old wartime aircraft like the Beaufighter, Mosquito and even the hallowed Spitfire, unless one had to actually fly and fight in them. They were simply the best technology available at the time, but that did not mean to say they

A big gun to put in a plane: This picture shows the complete Molins gun in its original anti-tank configuration. It all fitted into the Mosquito – somehow. The Molins Machine Company specialised in making cigarette vending machines before the war, and turning their wartime efforts to the manufacture of such a potent weapon seems somehow very appropriate.

were without faults or vices, or even that the men who had to fly them had to like them. Not all of them did. As far as the Mosquito was concerned, those huge un-silenced Merlin engines made for an extremely noisy and uncomfortable flight. They were tricky machines to taxi, difficult to get airborne safely, and even harder to land. They vibrated so badly in flight that it could sometimes be impossible to even read the instruments, and on top of it all the Mosquito had her famous wing-tip stalling characteristic always waiting to trap the unwary.

Until recent years when it was still possible to see a Mosquito performing at a British airshow, the sight and sound could be a magnificent one for a spectator. But it was a lot different for those who had to strap themselves into such a machine in 1945 and take it to war over a hostile ocean and a hostile country. Angus McIntosh was a Strike Wing pilot who survived the full nine months of operations with Banff Strike Wing. He stayed on in the RAF after the war, retiring with the rank of Group Captain. He had converted to the silky-smooth flight of jet-engined Gloster Meteor fighters immediately after being transferred from piston-engined Mosquitos – an experience that quickly demonstrated to him how hard his life had been as a Strike Wing Mosquito pilot.

He should know the difference better than most. Asked if he missed the old piston engine Mosquitos, his reply was unexpected, but at least honest.

"You've got to be kidding," he said, "they were noisy, dangerous buggers of things."

CHAPTER 5
THE MISSIONS

SEPTEMBER 1944 WAS A HEADY TIME for the Allies. Things were at last starting to look good on the European continent, with the German Wehrmacht in full retreat after the spectacular breakout from Normandy and the closing of the Falaise pocket on the western front. Meantime in the east, the Soviet Red Army's enormous *Operation Bagration* (which utterly dwarfed events on the western front) had come to a successful end with massive territorial gains and enormous losses inflicted on the Germans. In hindsight, all these momentous events seem to have gone to people's heads, with rampant speculation on the possibility of the war being over by Christmas 1944. Field Marshal Montgomery however, who was about to launch his infamous *Operation Market Garden*, would soon prove that the war still had a long way to go before it would be over.

Preparation: Unlike many of the staged ground shots taken at RAF Banff, this one was for real. With strike operations being halted only for the worst weather conditions, clearing snow off aircraft about to fly was vital in order that the aerodynamic properties were not affected.

The outriders: This fine study was taken in the spring of 1945 from inside a blister hangar at Banff and shows Mosquito KK-F, one of the ten "pool" aircraft used by 333 Squadron, prior to another mission over Norway searching for targets for the main Strike Wing.

Last sight of home: Mosquitos begin to form up in close formation in the circuit over Banff, with the village of Whitehills visible in the background. The forming-up of around 40-50 aircraft over the base was a sight many veterans say they will never forget. Neither would the residents of northern Aberdeenshire, as the wing made its way along the coast to Rattray Head to meet its Mustang escorts.

THE MISSIONS

Polish friends: A P-51 Mustang from number 315 (City of Deblin) Polish Fighter Squadron based at RAF Peterhead, tucks in close beside the Mosquito it is escorting. The irony of the last year of the war saw fighter squadrons posted to northern Scotland – previously seen as a "rest" posting – facing far stronger enemy fighter opposition over Norway than they would find over Germany itself by that time.

Nonetheless, spirits were high by the time the men and machines of Coastal Command gathered in the north-east of Scotland in early September 1944 to form the new Banff Strike Wing. But if this was the case, then just as at Arnhem, a harsh dose of reality was about to be administered. In the nine months that were remaining of the war, the new wing would undertake more than fifty combat operations where battle was joined with the enemy in one way or another. Despite the appearance of being in the ascendancy over the German war machine, Banff aircrew would be killed in over half of these operations. More than fifty aircraft from Banff would be lost during this period, fifteen of them at the hands of enemy fighters over Norway. Eighty-five men would die flying from Banff's runways, with many more wounded or shot down and captured. It soon became very obvious to all concerned, that the task the new Strike Wing faced was going to be no milk run.

Things got off to a slow start, despite the determination of everyone from the station commander downwards to get stuck in as quickly as possible. People and aircraft were still arriving at the base. Crews who had converted to Mosquitos from Beaufighters were still getting used to their new mounts. Others, like 235 Squadron, were practising using rockets for the first time. Meantime, all of them were getting to grips not only with flying

> **"NEWS OF THE MONTH"**
> Last pay night, F/Sgt Chew and Sgt. Roberts bought a car off the first man they met in a pub, on the one condition that it made it to the top of the hill from the town. It did.
> *Chocks Away, October 1944*

Under the radar: Banff Strike Wing aircraft from 235 Squadron speed across the North Sea at low level toward Norway. Most veterans claim that they maintained a height of 50 feet on outward-bound flights. At these heights, the ride was not only extremely bumpy, but also very dangerous, with almost no height for recovery if a problem suddenly arose with the aircraft.

The wrong kind of rockets: The ship under attack here is the 1,953 ton Rudolf Oldendorff, *which was sunk near Egersund on 9 October 1944. Explosive head rockets have already started the fires which eventually sank her. But lots of hits with these were needed, and it was realised that solid shot rockets would have punctured her hull and sunk her with less hits.*

THE MISSIONS

over the huge northern North Sea, but also with trying to find their way around the enormous fjord-indented coastline of Norway. The weather was also a problem, and the first two operational *Rovers* – armed patrols – got nowhere because of the unseasonably bad conditions. Finally, on the 14 September, the wing started shooting in anger with an operation off southern Norway near Kristiansand. In return for sinking a flakship, the wing lost a Beaufighter. They sank another one three days later, but these were relatively small fry, and not what the wing was after. More calls-offs were caused by the weather during September, until the wing finally caught and sank some meatier targets in the shape of a small convoy of merchant ships – precisely what they *were* after – in Askevold, although another Beaufighter was again lost to flak.

Eight operations were launched that September, although with only half of them resulting in ships being sunk. October and November saw a similar level of activity, with eight combat operations mounted during each month and some ten ships sunk, four of which were decent-sized merchantmen. The wing had by

Do it quickly: Attacking immediately was the best way to catch the flak defences off guard. Unfortunately, the deadly significance a single 333 Squadron Mosquito appearing overhead soon became recognised throughout Norway, and fully-alerted ships and their flak gunners were usually ready. Here, during the Sandefjord attack of 2 April 1945, the ship nearest the camera, the 5,154 ton Concordia, *is about to be sunk.*

Saturation fire: The full view of a picture detailed earlier shows how concentrated the fire brought to bear on a target could be. Here at Aalesund on the 17 March 1945, Mosquitos followed their standard practice of attacking either individually or in pairs, one after the other. Few of the thin-skinned merchant vessels could take such sustained punishment and most, like the 3,323 ton Iris *seen here, were quickly sent to the bottom.*

now clearly announced both its presence and its intentions in Norway, and the Germans reacted quickly by stopping daytime sailings, then going all-out to stop the Strike Wings as well. From December 1944 onwards, things were about to get a lot harder – for both sides.

The daytime sailing ban saw all merchant ships in Norwegian waters spending the daylight hours holed-up either in harbours or deep inside fjords. Ships which chose to berth in harbours could still be attacked and were only marginally better off than if they had been still at sea, since the shore-based flak could provide additional protection. On balance, of course, being in harbour meant that they were stationary, and a lot easier to attack and hit from the air.

Those ships choosing the latter option however, could gain a degree more safety by anchoring hard against the steep sides of the fjords, and although this did not guarantee them immunity from attack by the determined Strike Wings, it did mean that flak guns could be sited high up on the sides of the overlooking mountains to fire *down* on the attacking aircraft.

This is precisely what happened on the 5 December 1944 at Nordgulenfjord, and it proved to be a very one-sided battle. Three

THE MISSIONS

Overshoot: This 143 Squadron Mosquito has overshot the target with its rockets during an attack in Sandshamn, Sunnmore on March 23rd 1945. The 900 ton Lysaker *sports (like all Norwegian merchant ships at the time) large Norwegian flags on the side of her hull intended to persuade attacking aircraft to leave her alone. But they were all in German service and were always armed with flak gun positions.* Lysaker *was sunk in this attack, but raised in 1946, renamed the* Solskin *and sailed the world until scrapped in 1969. Three Mosquitos were lost on this day's operations, although the crew of one aircraft were captured.*

Deep in the fjords: This photograph from the gunner's cupola in a Beaufighter well illustrates the scale of the steep-sided fjords in which so many of the Strike Wing anti-shipping attacks were undertaken. The Beaufighters shown are dwarfed by the scenery, and only the smoke puffs from the rockets and the strikes on the target ship show that an attack is taking place.

squadrons – 143, 235 and 248 – formed the force that carried out the attack on four large German merchant ships which had been spotted anchored in the fjord by 333 Squadron outriders earlier in the day. Attacking the ships hard against the fjord walls demanded great flying skills and yet ultimately proved very unproductive. None of the ships were sunk or even seriously damaged, mainly because there was no flying room for the attacking aircraft to walk their fire to the targets before launching their cannon and rocket fire. They could not attack the ships side-on, because the steep-sided narrowness of the fjord denied the attacking aircraft any low-level flying space, so they were forced to try to hit the ships from the stern or slightly on the beam. None succeeded to any noticeable degree.

Meantime, the German flak gunners had themselves a field day. Although only one Mosquito was shot down into the fjord, no less than ten others were shot to pieces by flak. One was forced to divert to Sumburgh in the Shetlands on one engine, where it crash-landed and the pilot was killed. Three other Mosquitos had to limp home on one engine and land at the nearest airfield they could find, as did two others with other battle damage. Four damaged aircraft made it back to Banff with the rest of the wing. It had been

THE MISSIONS

Dalsafjord 1: On the same day that Lysaker *was sunk, other elements of the Strike Wing attacked this ship – the 7,854 ton* Rotenfels. *The ship was damaged but not sunk. Here, the camera ship makes its diving approach to the target – one already wreathed in the smoke and splashes of cannon and rocket fire. High above, flak bursts in the sky from shore batteries.*

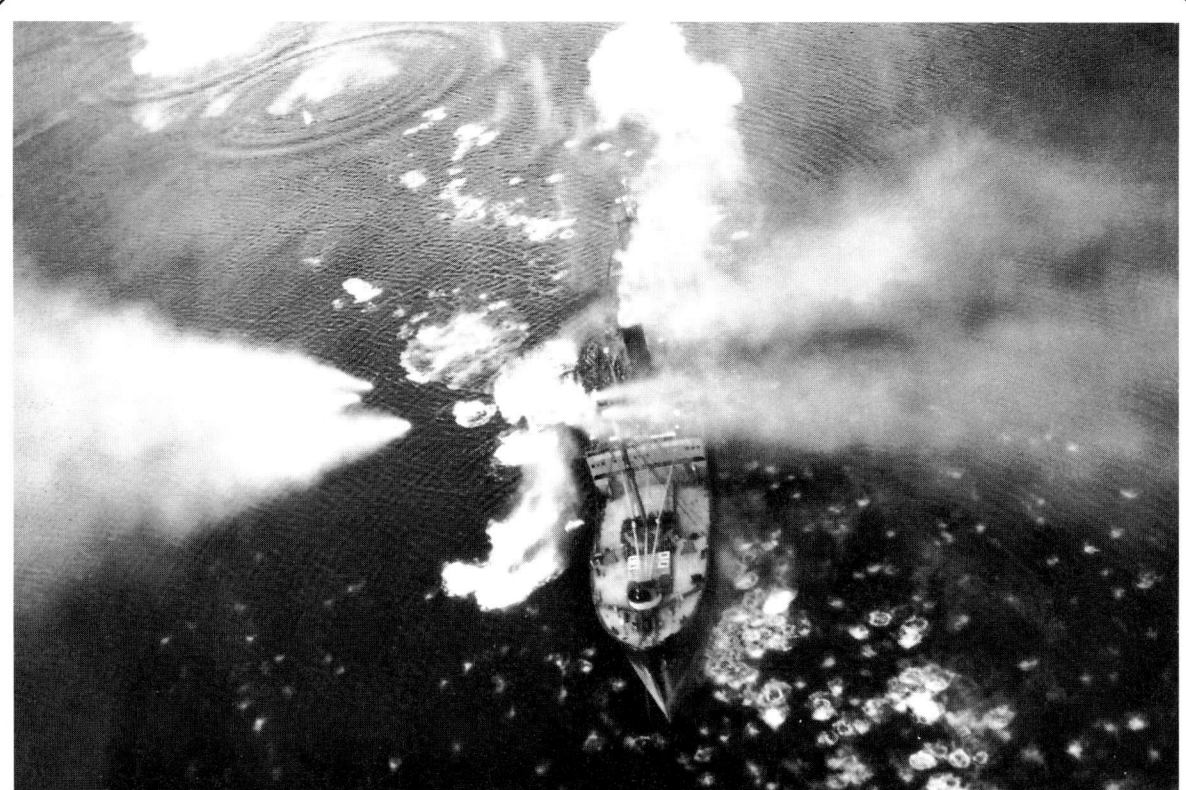

Dalsafjord 2: During this attack, the Mosquito of Squadron Leader Reid and his navigator Flying Officer Turner crashed into the fjord and exploded after being hit by flak, although the two sets of ripples seen here beyond the ship were not *caused by the crash – which has not taken place yet – but by a salvo of overshooting rockets. The sad sight of what an aircraft diving straight into a fjord actually looks like, can be seen in the next chapter.*

Mosquito down: On the 5 April 1945, Major Haakon Wenger, commander of the Norwegian Flight at Banff, was forced to belly land in Sweden in KK-E after being hit by flak from a convoy in the Kattegat. Somewhat unusually, the entire cockpit canopy seems to have been removed following the landing. Wenger and his navigator escaped back to Banff.

THE MISSIONS

a bad day at the office. But the month was still young. Ten full combat operations would take place in December, resulting in seven ships being sunk, five of which were large ore-carrying merchantmen.

Two days after the Nordgulenfjord mauling, the Strike Wings had a go at attacking a German fighter airfield. 25 Mosquitos from Banff, with 40 Beaufighters from Dallachy escorted by 12 Mustangs from Peterhead attacked Gossen airfield, only to be "bounced" by a dozen German Bf-109 and Fw-190 fighters. The Mustangs of 315 Squadron claimed to have shot down four Bf-109s. Two of the German Fw-190s collided with each other. Meantime, a Mustang, a Beaufighter and two Mosquitos were shot down. The wing would have another crack at Gossen airfield five days later, then give up airfield attacks as a bad idea and concentrate on shipping. These continued with strikes at Kraakhellesund and Flekkefjord, adding to the steadily rising tally of ships being sunk, but also to the wing's own losses.

> **"HEARD IN THE BUS QUEUE"**
> "Do you believe that dreadful story they are telling about Mabel?"
> "Of course I do. What is it?"
> *Chocks Away, April 1945*

No quarter given: The uncompromising nature of anti-shipping attacks is well illustrated during this attack in Hjeltefjord on the 23 October 1944. In this attack, the 220 ton harbour vessel Zick V5506 was sunk and the Merchant ship Biri damaged. The ships have sought shelter close into shore, but it has failed to save them from their fate.

Haugesund Harbour: The German merchant ship Eckenheim *in the process of being attacked and sunk while tied-up at the quay on the 21 October 1944. Flying Officers Driscoll and Hannant of 248 Squadron were killed in the attack when their Mosquito was hit by flak.*

A hat-trick of U-boats: The 9 April 1945 became a famous day for Banff Strike Wing, when no less than three U-boats were caught and sunk in the Kattegat. Two of the larger type IXC U-boats blew up, taking all hands and an RAF Film Unit Mosquito down with them. Here, a Mosquito churns-up the sea with its cannon and machine-gun fire as it finds the range and prepares to fire its rockets.

THE MISSIONS

Closing-in for the kill: This dramatic photograph, also taken during the 9 April U-boat killing spree in the Kattegat, conveys not only a sense of the speed of the attack, as the U-boat ploughs right through a walking line of cannon and machine-gun fire, but also just how low the aircraft taking the picture must have been flying. The top of a U-boat conning tower stood no more than 20 feet out of the water, yet this attacking Mosquito is almost level with it. The submarine is also very close, and cannon-fire damage to the planking on the after-deck can be seen, as well as the decidedly un-manned guns.

Don't look behind you: A scene that could strike fear into the hearts of many German aircrew during the Second World War, as a heavily-armed Mosquito approaches from astern. Taken from the dorsal gun position of an RAF Hudson, the picture shows the film unit Mosquito which was based at RAF Banff, which flew with the wing on operations until lost in action.

Rockets in return: A sequence of photographs from an attack by Banff Strike Wing on the 15 October 1944 at Lillesand, near the southern Norwegian port of Kristiansand. The vessel under attack here is the 426 ton Flakship Mosel Vp1605. *The crew, knowing their attackers will be passing over the ship at low level, have launched their own rockets vertically. These carried steel cables and were designed to bring down any attacking aircraft that flew into them.*

Retribution: These flakships were the Strike Wing's most dangerous adversary, other than enemy fighters, and were responsible for killing a large amount of Banff and Dallachy aircrew. The pilot of the Mosquito taking these pictures closes-in on the target with obvious determination, now striking the ship with the full force of his four 20mm cannons.

THE MISSIONS

The main target erupts: The flakship was escorting the 1,200 ton tanker Inger Johanne *from Oslo to Kristiansand. With a cargo of petroleum aboard, it was never going to take much to ensure her destruction at the hands of well-armed attackers. The cause of the explosion is obvious, with the two tell-tale puffs of smoke showing where a salvo of rockets have been launched and then found their mark. The guilty Mosquito has just flown out of shot.*

Finishing it off: Already on its run-in to target, a second Mosquito launches its rockets at the doomed petrol tanker. Things happened quickly during a shipping strike, and the timespan between this photograph and the previous one may have been as little as a second or two. On the bows of the tanker, a flak gun cupola can clearly be seen, although it is doubtful if it would have been either manned or used considering the nature of the cargo aboard.

On boxing day, the wing was back over Norway again, this time attacking shipping in Leirvik harbour when two dozen Bf-109 and Fw-190 fighters dived down on them. This time however, the wing was spread-out in the sky and the Mosquitos were able to take on the enemy fighters on more equal terms. Three enemy fighters went down for the loss of one Mosquito, although three others sustained damage and limped back to base. The onset of a ferocious winter over Scotland was about to slow down the operations and the sinkings for the next two months as far as Banff Strike Wing was concerned – but not stop them completely. Perhaps it had been better if they had. The German fighters were about to take a heavy toll on the Strike Wing. And the name of Leirvik, was about to pass into notoriety at RAF Banff.

The increasing presence of enemy fighters making determined attacks on the Strike Wing revealed itself as a taster of what was to come on the 11 January 1945 over Flekkefjord. A dozen Bf-109s and Fw-190s appeared from both north and south and a series of big dogfights ensued. One of the Tsetse Mosquitos began blasting away at the German aircraft with its huge 57mm anti-tank gun, which may explain the sudden departure of the enemy fighters into the safety of nearby cloud cover. Three German aircraft were seen to be shot down, with young Flight Lieutenant Noel Russell DFC, being credited with two of them. But once again, there was a price to pay. One Beaufighter and one Mosquito were lost, together with their crews. The Luftwaffe, in putting up such a fight, were succeeding in keeping the wing too busy fighting air battles to be able to sink any ships. Three days later, this point would be more forcibly made by the German fighter pilots.

On the 15 January, 1945, a formation of Mosquitos set off from Banff with specific instructions from 18 Group headquarters to

"CLUELESS CROSS"

The Most Ancient and Moronic Society breathlessly awards its highest honour to an A Flight rigger who blithely attempted to shave himself on a revolving propeller, and was only restrained from carrying out his death-defying act a second time by the implorations of a brother erk down on his bended knees. Modestly, the rigger then walked away from the aircraft by going round the back of the engine from the door, just like anyone else. Courage of this kind brings tears to the eyes.

Chocks Away, April 1945

THE MISSIONS

sink the 5,000 ton merchant ship *Claus Rickmers*, which the wing had damaged in Leirvik harbour some six days before. Speculation about the cargo on board the *Claus Rickmers* seems to have settled on the idea that it was Heavy Water, the main catalyst in the half-hearted German effort to produce an atomic bomb. This, however, was definitely not the cargo, as the entire manufacturing plant had been moved to Germany early in 1944 following the final USAAF bombing raid on the heavy water plant at Vermork in November 1943. What now seems more likely, is that some gung-ho staff officer at 18 Group headquarters at Pitreavie had simply demanded to see the word *sunk,* rather than merely *damaged,* typed next to the name of this large merchant ship.

Whatever the real reason, nine young Banff airmen would pay with their lives for this obsession. The problem was that the force which set out for Leirvik was a small one – only 16 aircraft – and that they did so without any fighter escort from Peterhead. Furthermore, the wing was showing a predictable streak, having recently attacked Leirvik twice. This time, the fighters were waiting. Although the wing sank a flak ship in the initial attack, they could not sink the *Claus Rickmers* because she was now firmly beached. When the fighters pounced, no fewer than five Mosquitos were quickly shot down. Among the men killed were some notable and highly popular personalities from the Strike Wing, including the French commander of 143 Squadron, Max Guedj,

Pillar of death: The Inger Johanne *veers away out of control with it's precious cargo of petrol already consumed in flames, before she eventually sank. Sixteen Norwegian crewmen died on the ship. Meanwhile, to the right of the burning tanker, the German flakship has been silenced and sits dead in the water, also burning.*

and the American pilot, Frederick Alexandre. Once again, the Tsetse Mosquitos opened-up with their big anti-tank guns, chasing off the attackers, but only after they had inflicted serious casualties on the wing. Rather incredibly, given the clear effects the Tsetse guns were having on the German fighter pilots, this was the last time they flew with the wing, and the aircraft were transferred south.

Life went on back at a sombre RAF Banff, but it was ten days before the wing struck over Norway again, sinking a couple of merchant ships in Edjfjord. On their return, two Mosquitos collided in the circuit over the base, killing one of the crews, although the pilot of the second aircraft, Wing Commander Gunnis, the 248 Squadron commander, somehow managed to land back at base with half of his starboard wing missing. Things seemed to be getting grimmer, and the weather was not helping either. In atrocious blizzard conditions, the Strike Wing still somehow managed to mount nine operations during that January and February, and to sink four merchant ships. But spring-time was coming for Banff Strike Wing, and in more ways than one. During March 1945, the wing moved up a gear and put into practice their increasing abilities by mounting no less than twelve operations and sinking ten ships. Even the German fighter attacks were beginning to thin out, with only two air battles between the wing and the Luftwaffe during that month, although as always, these resulted in losses for the Strike Wing Mosquitos and their escorting Peterhead Mustangs.

But the tide was definitely turning. An attack on shipping at Porsgrunn-Skien in the south of Norway on the 30 March had resulted in the sinking of no less than five large merchant ships for the loss of one Mosquito, which hit power cables strung across the river and crashed almost immediately into the edge of a nearby field. April would prove to be yet another ferocious month of fighting, with no less than 12 ships sunk by the wing, including four U-boats. Banff Strike Wing was now in the ascendancy, and had honed their ship-killing skills to perfection.

A successful attack on shipping and ship repair facilities at Sandefjord was followed by several days of happy hunting in the Kattegat, south of Norway, where the wing scored its first real success against U-boats, which had now been suicidally ordered to fight it out on the surface with any attacking aircraft. But still the steady losses of aircrew continued, and on the 11 April the enemy

THE MISSIONS

A private job by the boys: From the album of "Jack" Frost, this series of photographs show an attack on the lighthouse at Terningen, on the coast of Trøndelag, near the island of Hitra. The German keeper at this lighthouse always came out and started firing at the wing with a machine-gun as it flew overhead. Finally, the airmen got tired of it and the matter became, as Frost writes in his caption to these pictures: "A private job undertaken by the boys – and completed!". In reality, lighthouse attacks were fully authorised by the RAF in agreement with the Norwegian government in exile, since they were considered an aid to German shipping.

Closing in: Ranging shots from the machine-guns of a Mosquito throw puffs of smoke into the air around the lighthouse. As the aircraft roars in fast and almost level with it, the German lighthouse keeper has now become conspicuous by his sudden absence.

Take that: A 248 Squadron Tsetse *aircraft has found the range and let fly not only with a full salvo of twin-tiered rockets, but also with a 57mm round from its big anti-tank gun.*

Job done: Yet another Mosquito captures the moment when its ordnance found the mark. The wing was never shot at again from here. A new lighthouse was built on the site in 1958.

THE MISSIONS

After the battle: The rebuilt Terningen lighthouse today, which is now unmanned, but which may be visited and even lived in by visitors and tourists.

fighters put in one last appearance during a shipping strike on Porsgrunn. Here, the wing once again sent some merchant ships to the bottom – although on this occasion *only* four of them – before the air battle developed. One Mosquito was shot down, although it would prove to be the last one lost to German fighters.

On the 19 April the wing bagged another U-boat in the Kattegat and damaged a second one. It seemed that Banff Strike Wing now ruled the skies over Scandinavia. As if to emphasise just how much the tables had turned, the wing was now about to do some serious shooting-down of aircraft themselves.

On the 21 April, 1945, Banff Strike Wing unwittingly made a bit of history. On their return from an unusually unsuccessful foray into the Kattegat, the wing – comprising some 45 Mosquitos – was some 150 miles off the northern Aberdeenshire coast when it ran into a formation of German torpedo bombers heading for their own traditional anti-shipping hunting grounds off Rattray Head. The 24 Mustangs that had been escorting the wing had been given permission to race home to Peterhead, where a party was planned in the officers mess for that evening. Not that their absence made much difference to the outcome.

Nine Junkers Ju-88 aircraft from II/KG26, together with nine of the newer Junkers Ju-188s from III/KG26 were armed with a torpedo under each inboard wing. When the big force of Mosquitos saw them, they went straight into the attack and claimed nine bombers as shot down and several more as probables. This was unusual in itself. Throughout the war, on both sides, aircrew had always been guilty of over-inflating their claims for shot-down aircraft. This time, the opposite was the case. Post war, it was established that only four aircraft from the German formation had managed to return to Norway, where all of them had crash-landed at various bases. None of the rest were ever seen again, which meant that the wing had actually shot down 14 aircraft. What made this short and brutal action so unique, is that this was the last air attack mounted by the Luftwaffe in World War

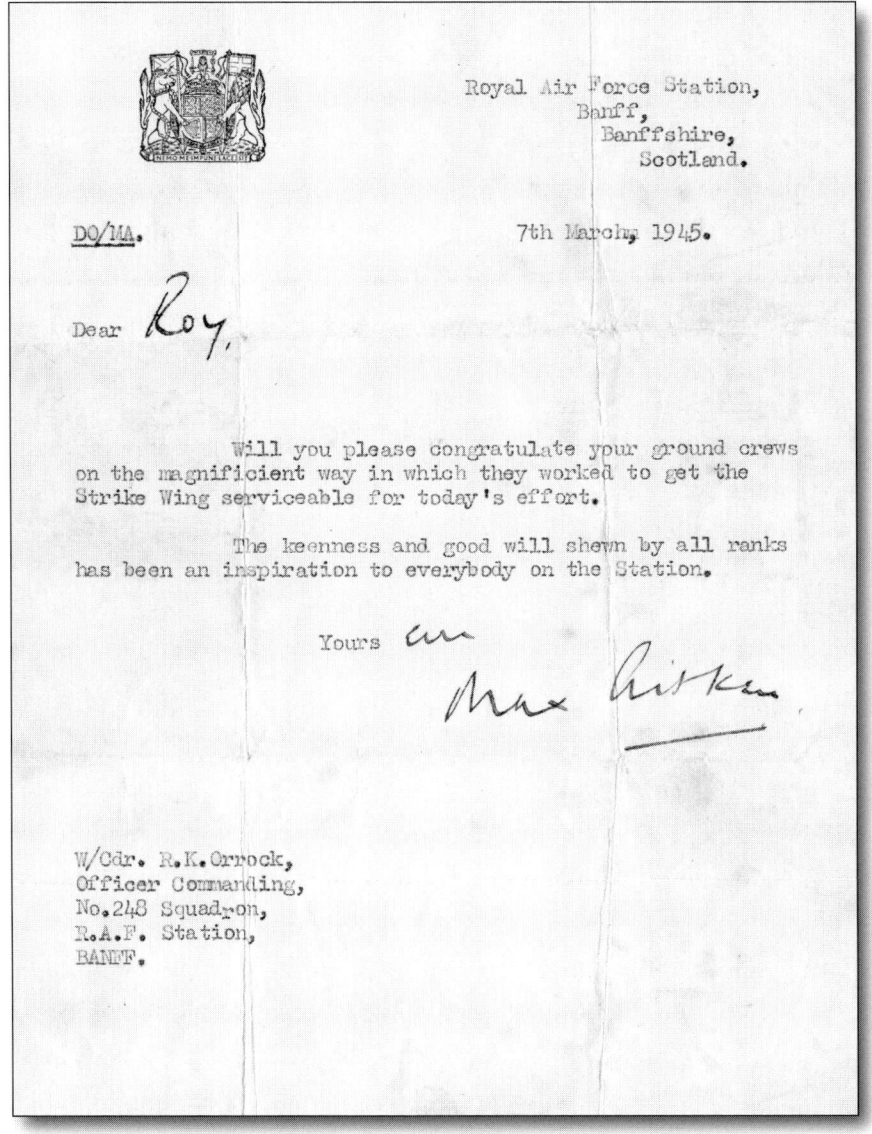

Thanks boys: Max Aitken displays his leadership with a post-strike letter to the commander of 248 Squadron. Ten days later, the squadron would be looking for a new commander, when Roy Orrock and his navigator were shot down and captured at Aalesund.

THE MISSIONS

Two. If that wasn't significant enough, it was also the last air battle ever fought in the skies of northern Europe.

The momentous month of May 1945, soon arrived. On the 2 May, the first of the wing's last two wartime missions was mounted, when some 27 Mosquitos – unescorted by fighters – headed back to the Kattegat to see what they could find. By the time they returned, another U-boat and a minesweeper could be added to the big tally board on the wall of the operations room of ships sunk, together with another U-boat damaged.

Two days later, the Strike Wing's final combat took place over the Kattegat. No less than 41 Mosquitos were escorted by eighteen Mustangs from Peterhead, with three ASR Warwicks from Banff tagging along to drop lifeboats to any crews who might have to ditch. The war, everyone knew, was on its last legs and nobody wanted to risk their lives needlessly at this stage. Nonetheless, it was still officially a shooting war, and although the wing sank their last big merchant ship that day – the *Wolfgang L.M. Russ* – and damaged another, several aircraft were hit by the intense flak barrage from these ships. Four of the Mustang escorts from number 19 Squadron failed to return, with two of the pilots killed. Two Mosquitos were so badly damaged that they also failed to return to Banff, both crash-landing in Sweden. The Mosquito of Flight Lieutenant Thorburn of 235 squadron hit a stone wall on landing, killing the pilot. He was to be the last man killed in action with Banff Strike Wing.

Symbolically, the Strike Wing flew one final patrol on the last day of the war.

But the combat missions – and the death and destruction – had come to an end.

CHAPTER 6
THE MISSING

FIFTY-SIX YEARS TO THE DAY after he was killed over Leirvik, Commandante Max Guedj, formerly known as Wing Commander "Maurice" DSO, DFC and bar, was posthumously honoured in France by having a Paris street named after him - the *Esplanade Max Guedj*.

Few of the eighty-four other men who died flying with Banff Strike Wing have been quite so spectacularly honoured. For most of these casualties of war, a granite headstone in a quiet corner of a cemetery in Norway or north-east Scotland is the sole marker of their time on earth. For many, even this was not possible and their bodies remain where they fell, either deep beneath the surface of a Norwegian fjord or somewhere out in the North Sea. It would be impossible to describe the fate of each of these brave young men here, so instead a full roll of honour of those who died flying with Banff Strike Wing is provided at the end of this book. This roll of honour can also be seen in the Book of Remembrance at St Mary's

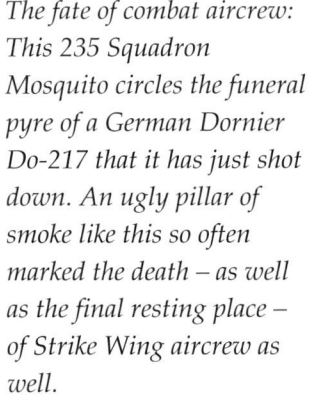

The fate of combat aircrew: This 235 Squadron Mosquito circles the funeral pyre of a German Dornier Do-217 that it has just shot down. An ugly pillar of smoke like this so often marked the death – as well as the final resting place – of Strike Wing aircrew as well.

THE MISSING

Askevold attack 1. It is hard to imagine a more beautiful place to violate with a battle. The scene for this sequence of photographs is Askevold, some sixty miles north of Bergen, on a beautiful afternoon on the 19 September 1944. Yet death fills these images. A small convoy of merchantmen en route from Hamburg to Tromso are spotted and the attack begins.

Askevold attack 2. Taking a battering from Flying Officer Frost's guns is the 1,364 ton merchant ship Lynx, *with the Norwegian flags emblazoned on her hull having no effect on Frost's determination to sink her. Moments later, a 37mm flak shell exploded in his cockpit and badly wounded him, leading to his long one-engined flight all the way back to Banff.*

Askevold attack 3. The death of the Lynx *is captured for posterity by the low-flying aircraft that probably administered the killer blow with the attack captured here. The rockets have clearly found their mark and an explosion erupts on the foredeck. She soon sank into the fjord.*

THE MISSING

Askevold attack 4. Under determined attack, another ship in the same convoy was the 937 ton merchant ship Ursa, *seen here turning hard to port at full speed in a manoeuvre which no doubt saved her. In addition to the* Lynx, *the large merchantman* Tyrifjord, *was also sunk in this attack. But the death and destruction was not all one-sided.*

Askevold attack 5. One of our aircraft is missing. So runs the caption in David Frost's personal photo album. Beaufighter "L" of 144 Squadron has just plunged straight into the fjord after being hit by flak while attacking the ship hidden by smoke on the left of the picture. The pilot, Flight Sergeant Hossack and his navigator Warrant Officer Wicks, were both killed.

Film Unit Casualties: Flight Lieutenant Jones and his navigator Flying Officer Newell pose by their specially-modified Mosquito. This was a dedicated RAF Film Unit aircraft with a movie camera mounted in the nose above the machine guns, which flew with the wing operationally, as can be testified by the symbols painted below the cockpit denoting four ships and a lighthouse attacked. On the 9 April 1945, this crew took their dedication to their task too far, when they followed a Mosquito making a low-level rocket attack on a U-boat in the Kattegat. As they flew over the U-boat, it exploded and their Mosquito was caught in the blast and crashed into the sea, killing both men.

Church in Banff, which was donated by the RAF Banff Strike Wing Memorial Trust. That these men were buried where they fell overseas is evidenced by the cluster of RAF graves at the town cemetery at Colleonard Road in Banff. Of the eighteen graves here, only six were from the Strike Wing. The rest of the RAF men who lie here – like the Strike Wing men who share this corner of the graveyard with them – were all casualties of the all-too-frequent flying accidents and crashes that took place on or around the airfield out at Boyndie.

One of the Strike Wing airmen who lies here, twenty-two year old Flying Officer Ernest Raymond Davey, a Canadian pilot with 404 Squadron, gained a degree of posthumous fame in the decades after he died, with a poem he wrote one day at RAF Banff. Born in London, Ontario on 25 November 1921, Davey was typical of the thousands of young men who flocked to the United Kingdom from

"MONTHLY NEWS FLASHES"

We heard the other day, a bod saying to another bod, "I say, didn't I meet you somewhere in the South of France once?" It turns out they did, and were old friends. F/Sgts Chew and Couttie, returned to the Squadron after many moons and a very interesting Cook's Tour of a certain part of the Continent which shall remain nameless. Congratulations and welcome back.

Chocks Away, November 1944

THE MISSING

all over the British Commonwealth during the Second World War. The second of five children, Davey earned the nickname "Bus" in childhood for some unknown reason, and enlisted in the Royal Canadian Air Force in May 1940 at the age of eighteen. In February 1943, after comprehensive training in his native Canada, "Bus" gained his flying wings, and was then commissioned as an officer in May the same year. His commemorative photograph shows a handsome young man sporting the almost obligatory Clarke Gable moustache of that era. In the summer of 1944, Flying Officer Ernest Raymond Davey was finally shipped-out to Europe, ready to go to war.

Upon arrival, he was thrown straight into the deep end with a posting to 404 (Buffalo) Squadron, an operational Canadian unit, where "Bus" caught the tail-end of the squadron's post D-Day activities hitting shipping in western France. Then it was straight up to northern Scotland, where 404 Squadron operated as part of Banff Strike Wing before moving to Dallachy in late October. Davey, however, never made it that far. Like so many of his generation, his odds of survival as the pilot of a combat aircraft, must have weighed heavily on his intelligent young mind. One day at Banff, he went back to his billet and quietly composed his famous poem, now known by the title of *An Airman's Prayer*:

> *Almighty and all-present power,*
> *short is the prayer I make to Thee;*
> *I do not ask in battle hour,*
> *for any shield to cover me.*
> *The vast unalterable way,*
> *from which the stars do not depart,*
> *may not be turned aside to stay*
> *the bullet flying to my heart.*
> *I ask no help to strike my foe;*
> *I seek no petty victory here.*
> *The enemy I hate, I know to Thee is dear.*
> *But this I pray: be at my side,*
> *when death is drawing through the sky;*
> *Almighty God who also died,*
> *teach me the way that I should die.*

Although Davey clearly expected that his death – if it came – would be as a result of an enemy bullet, the manner of his passing

Wing Commander "Maurice" DSO, DFC and bar: The name adopted by Commandante Max Guedj, a French pilot in the RAF who wanted to protect the identity of his family in occupied France. A popular leader of 143 Squadron, he was shot down and killed in the big air battle with German fighters over Leirvik on the 15 January 1945. On the 15 January 2001, a street in Paris named the Esplanade Max Guedj *was officially inaugurated in his honour.*

Fatal hit. The official caption for this photograph claims that the Beaufighter seen in the picture has just been hit and crashed immediately afterwards. The location is quoted as Breivgen, Fedefjord on 26 April 1945. The smoke trail on the right is from an anti-aircraft rocket trailing a cable, a device often used by German-controlled shipping in Norway.

Victim of the Leirvik battle: This Mosquito was also shot down in the battle over Leirvik that day in January 1945. Pilot Flight Sergeant Morton-Moncrieff and his navigator Flight Sergeant Cash were both killed in this aircraft, seen here fully armed in flight over Banffshire.

was rather different. When forming-up in the circuit over Banff before a strike operation on the 2 October, 1944, Davey's Beaufighter collided with another 404 Beaufighter flown by Flying Officer Long. Both aircraft were flying at around 2,000 feet at the time, and immediately plunged into the ground beside Wellhead Farm near Portsoy. All four aircrew were killed instantly. James Wilson was a schoolboy at Portsoy who witnessed the collision, particularly the "strange contortions" of the severed tail of one of the aircraft, as it "fluttered down out of the sky." It was a sad burial service at the cemetery in Banff the day these four young men were laid to rest. Back at the airfield, the unpleasant job of sorting out the mens' personal effects was being undertaken, when Davey's poem was uncovered. It became a fitting tribute to all of his generation.

Davey had died a long way from his home in Canada, and for so many of the relatives of men who hailed from all over the world, a pilgrimage to their graves in distant Scotland was often never possible. They had come from Australia, New Zealand and Canada – as they always had done in time of war. Yet not all of the men who fought and died at Banff were from the Commonwealth or even from the British home nations. Many had come from other countries, for their own reasons – but especially the Norwegians, who absolutely relished the chance to fight as free men over their occupied home country. Nine of them died doing precisely this from RAF Banff. Other men who fought had different motivations. Typical of the young Americans who joined the war before their own country did, was Freddie Alexandre from New York, who had joined the RAF in 1940. Once his country was also at war, he adopted the olive brown uniform of a Lieutenant in the United States Army Air Force, although he continued to fly

Flight Sergeant Frank Chew: Another casualty of the dogfight with nine Focke-Wulf Fw-190 fighters over Leirvik on the 15 January 1945, was young 235 pilot Frank Chew. His aircraft was one of five Mosquitos shot down that day. Chew's machine plunged into the fjord taking its pilot down with it. His navigator, Flight Sergeant Couttie, escaped and survived.

> **"CLUELESS CROSS"**
> The Most Ancient and Moronic Society bestirs itself this month to hurl the medallion unerringly at an A Flight sergeant for meticulous non-observation of details. When a pilot reported a mag drop the sergeant, with practically no reluctance, stomped out, started up the engine, belted it, tested switches – but found no mag drop. He switched off the engine and made his way to his office, muttering about the pilot's lack of ancestry. All at once, he realised he had run up aircraft E instead of aircraft L.
>
> *Chocks Away, Victory Edition, May 1945*

Lieutenant Rolf Leithe: All losses were tragic, but the death of young Norwegian pilot Rolf Leithe seemed particularly so, since it was within sight of his own 333 Squadron ground crews, who were powerless to help. During an air test on the 22 March 1945, Leithe was forced to make an emergency landing in a field near the main A98 Fraserburgh to Inverness road, very close to billets occupied by 333 Squadron. Although his navigator was thrown clear, Leithe's seat buckled under him and trapped his legs as the aircraft started to burn. Ole Inge Lindaas was only 19 years old when he watched the scene, and fifty years later could still recall Leithe's dreadful screams as he burned to death.

Lieutenant Rolf Leithe: The Norwegian pilot might have made a successful crash landing had his aircraft not struck this stone field dyke, which ripped the plywood machine apart and started the fire that killed him. The gouges in the grass from the aircraft's propellers can be clearly seen, as can the partially ruined dyke. With sad irony, the small field that this young man's tragedy took place in lies adjacent to the present-day site of the Banff Strike Wing Memorial. The spot where this wreckage lies, was used for one day only as a temporary car park for the memorial unveiling ceremony in 1989. For a brief moment during the flypast that day, many of the spectators were convinced that Tony Craig, the pilot of the Mosquito display aircraft, was about to crash into precisely the same field.

Christmas 1944: In the olde worlde Nissen hut of the officers mess at RAF Banff, Max Aitken entertains fellow officers and invited guests. On the left in the kilt is the local senior police officer, Chief Constable George Strath, with whom Aitken enjoyed a brief friendship at Banff, and which proved useful for getting wayward service personnel out of trouble. On the right is 248 Squadron Commander H.H.K. Gunnis, who would soon have a lucky escape in a mid-air collision over Banff. Next to Gunnis with a tankard is Squadron Leader David Pritchard, who stands next to the suave American pilot Frederick Alexandre, who would be killed less than three weeks after this picture was taken.

with the RAF as a flight commander in 143 Squadron. Suave and sophisticated, he was much admired by his fellow aircrew at Banff, and was all the more missed when he became a casualty of the air battle over Leirvik on the 15 January 1944.

Another young man who died that day over Leirvik, was Flight Sergeant Frank Chew from 235 Squadron. Frank had already had quite a war. On the 12 August 1944, Chew and his navigator had been shot down off the Gironde estuary in western France. Picked-up by an armed German trawler, both men were taken to the port of Royan, where a German naval officer proceeded to beat the two men in a savage temper. By now, Patton's armies were approaching, and the Germans were forced to keep their captives on the move. On one occasion, the trucks transporting these and other Allied POWs stopped for a break, and as the German guards lay relaxing in a group together in the sunshine, a Frenchman cycled past, waving at the Germans with loud cries of *Bonjour! Bonjour!* Frank Chew had immediately felt a little uneasy at this, and his suspicions were confirmed when the French cyclist uncovered a machine gun and began mowing down the nearest German guards, before speeding away on his cycle before the surviving guards could react.

> **"IN FEAR AND TREMBLING"**
> The old ship's cannon by the bus stop in Low Street in Banff is irremovable. Nor will 30 men, even aided by F/Sgt Smallwood standing on the barrel, urging them on with cries of "Two! Six!" make any impression on it.
> *Chocks Away, Victory Edition, May 1945*

Jack Frost's on one again: Flying Officer David Frost once more brings a Mosquito home across the North Sea on one engine, after being hit by flak over Norway. Although the Mosquito could fly perfectly well on one engine, it was a different matter if the second one then failed. The decision to head back to base over the cold North Sea in a crippled aircraft was not one that could be taken lightly. Many crews took the easier option and crossed the border into neutral Sweden to crash-land there.

Knowing that they were fleeing before the advancing American forces, Chew and his fellow prisoners feared that they were going to be herded all the way to Germany, and contrived to make themselves sick en-masse. Happy to be rid of them, the guards deposited them all into the custody of the local hospital at Angouleme, where the Maquis took control after the German occupying forces left the town on the 1 September. Thereafter, Frank enjoyed some superb French food and wine amid the glorious weather and scenery for a couple of days, before an RAF Dakota arrived and deposited him back in London on the 3 September, wearing the German boots he'd obtained to replace the pair lost when he'd ditched his aircraft. After a period of leave, Frank returned to 235 Squadron in the cooler surroundings of Banff to resume his duties as a Mosquito pilot. Despite his exploits and his popularity on the station, Chew never became an officer (many working-class NCOs refused a commission) and remained a Flight Sergeant until his death. On that fateful 15 January, Frank Chew went down with his aircraft after it crashed in the fjord at Leirvik. His navigator, Flight Sergeant Couttie, somehow got out and survived, spending the rest of the war as a POW. Frank's body was later recovered from the wreck of his Mosquito and buried –

THE MISSING

like so many of the Banff Strike Wing casualties of that day – at Mollendal cemetery.

Another man who now lies in a Norwegian cemetery a long way from home is Australian pilot Dick Atkinson. Thirty-two year old Wing Commander Richard Ashley Atkinson, DSO, DFC and bar, became the commander of 235 Squadron in October 1944 and was described by the squadron's magazine *Chocks Away*, as; "A man of few words but much experience". Born in Emmaville, New South Wales in 1913, Dick had recently become a father, and his baby son William and 20 year-old wife Joan, travelled north to Banff in late September 1944. Mother and son found lodgings with the local cooper and his wife at Distillery Cottages at Inverboyndie, a mile or so to the east of the airfield. At first, the Atkinsons were under the impression that their landlords spoke Gaelic, although this in fact was the almost impenetrable dialect (at least, for non-locals) of the English language known as Doric. Nonetheless, tenants and landlords bonded well, and the kindness of the latter to Joan in her darkest hour is testament to the fact. A month before he died, Dick Atkinson had been introduced to William Shakespeare in the form of *Hamlet* at His Majesty's Theatre in Aberdeen – an experience he had thoroughly enjoyed, stating in his letters home that he had; "sat on the edge of my seat for the whole three hours." In that last letter, Atkinson had spoken of his baby son in the proud way that any father would: "Bill is 24 inches long, so has grown four inches since birth, so should be a husky brute. I'm not overkeen on having a son who overtops me, but Joan likes the idea of having a six footer, dark and brawny, in the family."

Flying Officer E.J. Fletcher: Inevitably, this young 235 Squadron pilot was known as "Smiler". On Boxing Day, 1944, Fletcher was flying Mosquito "G" of 235 Squadron when he was shot down by enemy fighters over Leirvik. Both Fletcher and his navigator, Flying Officer Watson, were killed.

Porsgrunn-Skien-1: The following sequence of photographs are from the strike on Porsgrunn-Skien on the 30 March 1945, mentioned in the introduction. Flight Lieutenant William Knowles and his navigator Flight Sergeant Thomas were flying aircraft "T" of 235 Squadron when they dived down to attack the target and flew into high-tension cables strung across the river. The flash in the top left of the picture is the moment that their aircraft hit the ground just beyond the target and exploded.

Porsgrunn-Skien-2: These photographs are from the David Frost collection, and Frost has highlighted the location of the towers carrying the high-tension cables on this print. Frost's navigator was operating the camera, shooting one picture off after another, with this picture taken only seconds after the previous one. Knowles and his navigator died instantly in the crash.

Porsgrunn-Skien-3: As David Frost flies over the target, he also passes close to the crash site of Knowles and Thomas, and navigator Fuller zooms-in on the fireball now rising from the crash site. Meantime, the attack went on, and as if in retribution no less than five large merchant ships were sunk in this, the most successful single attack by the Strike Wing.

THE MISSING

Bill Atkinson would indeed slightly "overtop" his father at five feet eleven, although Dick Atkinson would not live long enough to see any of it. Shot down over Askvoll on the 13 December 1944, he died with his navigator, Flying Officer Upton, in the icy waters of the fjord. From then on, the links between a part of Australia and this part of Norway would be unbreakable. Ten years after Dick Atkinson was killed there, his father went to Askvoll and set up an engineering scholarship for local students as a memorial to both his sons (Dick's brother Tony, had been killed in a bomber over Magdeburg in Germany). The Atkinson family still regularly return, maintaining strong links with the people of Askvoll, who continue to honour the memory of the Mosquito crew who crashed and died there.

For twenty-year old Joan Atkinson, her husband's death suddenly left her all alone with a baby thousands of miles from home at the height of a global war. Joan claims that she knew she had lost her husband when the wing returned from Norway later that day. As a matter of routine, Dick and his fellow 235 Squadron pilots would "buzz" the lodgings at Distillery Cottages to let her know he was safely home. Dick himself – provided his aircraft was undamaged by combat – would usually perform a victory roll over the cottage.

That night, none of the returning aircraft came near the cottage, and as Joan heard them coming home to land without the usual low-level overflight, she had instinctively realised that her husband was dead. Max Aitken – displaying his usual immense leadership skills – had proved a tower of strength to the devastated young mother. Despite severe restrictions on civilian travel, he'd organised a priority pass for the heartbroken widow and her infant on a train to London, where she sat out the remainder of the war with one of Dick's relatives in St Albans. Almost eight months after her husband had been killed, and after an eight week voyage on a crowded ship, young Mrs Joan Atkinson and her baby son arrived in Sydney, Australia, just as the war against Japan came to an end.

Wing Commander Richard Ashley Atkinson, DSO, DFC and Bar: Dick Atkinson was the quiet but popular Australian commander of 235 Squadron, who left a wife and young baby in lodgings at Banff when he and his navigator Flying Officer Upton were killed at Ejdsfjord, south of Askevoll on 13 December 1944. The wing of Atkinson's Mosquito was hit by flak and set on fire. When he tried to turn the aircraft, the weakened wing sheared off and the aircraft plunged into the waters of the fjord.

A little part of Canada: The grave in Banff Cemetery of the Canadian pilot and poet, Ernest Raymond Davey, who wrote his now famous wartime poem while based at RAF Banff with 404 Squadron. Instead of a bullet to his heart, he died aged only 22 near Wellhead Farm, Portsoy, after a mid-air collision with another Beaufighter on take-off.

125

Thanksgiving: On VE Day, almost everyone from RAF Banff who could do so, travelled into the town of Banff itself and paraded en-masse in the big car park of St Mary's Church. They often paraded here for church services, since there were no such facilities on the airfield, and on this most emotional of days for all who lived to see it, they crammed St Mary's to capacity for a heartfelt service of thanksgiving.

Chocks Away - Victory Edition: The 235 Squadron magazine produced at Banff in May 1945 was a particularly poignant one, containing a mixture of both the usual forced service humour as well as the more profound thoughts of writers who had done so much themselves to achieve the victory that now seemed to overwhelm them with it's sudden finality and uncertainty. Uppermost in most minds, seemed to be the memories of the friends and crewmates who had lost their lives in the process of achieving this momentous victory.

THE MISSING

Like Dick Atkinson at Askvoll in Norway, some are remembered better than others. Ernest Davey has found immortality with his poem. Max Guedj has his street in Paris. All of them, would probably have preferred a long and happy life instead.

Or so it would seem to us in the present day. For all these men shared some common values – they lived in a more idealistic era and believed fiercely in the war they were fighting. To an extent, most were reconciled to the possibility that they might die fighting it. Some of them had very personal reasons for doing so. Perhaps Max Guedj illustrates this best. Born a Jew in Tunisia in 1913, Max had more than one reason to want to fight the Germans. But the fact that his Jewish family remained in occupied France while he fought against their oppressors, placed them in as much danger as he faced in combat. By adopting the pseudonym of *Maurice,* Max Guedj sought to protect his family from the terrible reprisals that the SS or Gestapo would have been sure to take upon them, had his real name been as widely publicised as his pseudonym. So he fought in anonymity to try to win their freedom. Even after France was liberated, Max Guedj kept on fighting the Germans to the end. This selfless dedication is something that his own nation has now made sure he will always be remembered for.

Names carved on memorials and street signs are all very well, though. Such tributes can never replace a loved one that has been lost. In an epitaph to Dick Atkinson written for his wife Joan, the poet Sydney Goodsir Smith perfectly sums-up this aching sense of loss;

> *There are no words of monumental praise,*
> *for him of whom a lass would say;*
> *"My eagle, oh my darling is asleep,*
> *dead is my love, my bright one's gone",*
> *and Christ, what can a monument ever speak?*
> *That he was noble, fearless, would it make him?*
> *Och, heap the unkept cairn upon the unkept grave.*
> *The heart knows more than monuments can raise*

The last remains at Banff: Some of the recovered wreckage from the Mosquito of Flight Lieutenant D.B. Douglas, which crashed into Hopetoun Farmhouse on the edge of RAF Banff in January 1945. The cottage remained in ruins after the crash until finally demolished in 1987. The excavator doing the work that day pulled out these propeller blades, undercarriage legs and large amounts of other debris, including a quantity of live 20mm ammunition.

CHAPTER 7
THE MEMORY

RAF BANFF, together with the squadrons, the aircraft and the buildings, were nothing more than tools of war. They were disposable. The people were the important part. It was only natural therefore, that from the moment the war had ended in victory over Nazi Germany, these highly expensive tools and facilities were indeed disposed of – and quickly. On the same month that the war in Europe ended, three Banff-based squadrons ceased to exist after being disbanded. All went on the same day, the 25 May 1945. Numbers 143 and 144 Squadrons, as well as the Canadian 404 Squadron, slipped into history. The aircraft went south into storage, the ground crews were demobbed, and everyone began to go home. The new peacetime world was on the move and changes were rapidly taking place. Even Max Aitken hurried back to London to stand as a Conservative candidate for

Demobbed: This overflight photograph of the southern end of RAF Banff taken in 1946, shows an intact yet abandoned airfield - immediately before a public auction here saw most of the demountable buildings sold off and removed, mostly for local farm use.

THE MEMORY

the London constituency of Holborn, which he duly won in the General Election held on the 6 July, 1945, although he would not serve a second term and followed his father into the *Express* newspaper empire.

Back at Banff, meantime, the airfield was emptying of people and planes. Perhaps the sweetest homecoming of them all must have been for the Norwegians of 333 Squadron "B" Flight. The day after the first three Banff squadrons were disbanded, the Norwegian flight was renamed 334 Squadron, Royal Norwegian Air Force, in recognition of their individual identity and achievements. They flew their Mosquitos back across the North Sea one last time to land in triumph at Gardermoen airfield near Oslo. Today, they are based at Andoya Air Station in Norway, operating Lockheed P-3C Orion maritime patrol aircraft. While the Norwegians were busy packing up and Max Aitken was becoming a Member of Parliament, 235 Squadron had bitten the dust at Banff. Meanwhile, 248 Squadron had moved south to Chivenor the month before, although they too were disbanded a year later. Apart from the renamed Norwegians, the only surviving Banff squadron is the Canadian 404 Squadron, which was reformed in 1951 back in Canada at RCAF Greenwood. Like the Norwegians, it too is now a maritime patrol outfit and flying basically the same aircraft in the shape of the Lockheed CP-140 Aurora.

No squadrons exist in the present-day RAF bearing the identity of any of the Banff Strike Wing squadrons, although an Air Training Corps squadron in England is now numbered 144 Squadron. Sadly, although they use a variation on the squadron's original wartime badge, there is no mention whatsoever of their

The Famous Commander: Max Aitken was one of the main reasons why the story of Banff Strike Wing did not completely sink without trace in the post-war years. The son of Lord Beaverbrook went on to inherit his father's Express *newspaper empire, yet never lost touch with Banff, returning on several occasions. Sadly, he did not survive to see the memorial being unveiled in memory of the Strike Wing he commanded at the wartime airfield.*

"WANT TO BUY AN AERODROME?"
This desirable freehold aerodrome, complete with all its accessories, including aeroplanes, transport, servicing units and living quarters, is hereby offered for sale. All the property is available in proper working order, and if required the purchase can be extended to include the contracts of all of the personnel employed. Applications, this magazine, from April 14th. (Editor goes on leave).

Chocks Away, April 1945

Movie stars: Anxious to film the crews and the aircraft before they all dispersed at the end of the war, the RAF Film Unit set to work recreating certain scenes using the crews of the Banff and Dallachy Strike Wings themselves. Here, Wing Commander Tony Gadd does his best movie star impersonation for the documentary The Shipbusters, *which used real combat footage to tell the Strike Wing story.*

A Mosquito returns: In June 1976, the silver-painted Strathallan collection Mosquito RS712 once more filled the skies over Banff airfield with the sound of Merlin engines, before landing to inaugurate the newly reopened airfield for the Banff Flying Club. This Mosquito has since been moved to the United States, and none now fly anywhere in Europe.

THE MEMORY

illustrious namesakes on their squadron's website. The same seems to be true of the only other existing UK unit with a direct connection to RAF Banff, which is again an ATC squadron. No.1296 Squadron was formed at Banff in 1944 and operated from a Nissen hut on the airfield, providing would-be future aircrew with air experience flights in Avro Ansons. Several former cadets remember flying from the airfield, and the guided tours they were given around the Strike Wing aircraft and the base facilities. Without a home after RAF Banff closed, the squadron moved to a new hall in nearby Turriff, where this writer was a member during the 1970s, although no apparent awareness of the squadron's legacy was ever evident then or now.

After the squadrons came the now-empty airfield, which was put on to a care and maintenance basis before being closed down a year after the war ended. As with most wartime airfields, the land reverted to the original owners, in this case the Earl of Seafield's Estates. The custom in Scotland in any displenishment situation is to conduct a *Roup* (auction) on the site and sell anything that can be moved. In the austere post-war years, this was not an opportunity to be missed for hard-pressed farmers and local business. All three of the big steel T-2 hangars were sold off, dismantled and removed by the new owners, as were the blister hangars, which made excellent farm buildings and barns. One example moved to within sight of the airfield, and remained in-

Bayhound Leader returns: Thirty years after he left, Sir Max Aitken returned to Banff to open the premises of Banff Flying Club. While this group photo was being taken, event organiser David Morgan was desperately trying to sort out a slight oversight, by borrowing a generator from RAF Lossiemouth in order to restart the Mosquito's engines. He eventually got one.

Reunited with the boss: Irishman Paddy Lyttle was a ground crewman at RAF Banff from 1944 to 1945. When the war ended, he stayed on in the town. Here, he is reunited with Sir Max Aitken at the airfield on the 2 June 1976. Aitken sent him this picture afterwards.

Priceless artefact: The few surviving 235 Squadron magazines are now very rare items indeed. Produced for light-hearted banter at the time, they are now like a window into another age.

situ on a farm at Hilton until the turn of the century – not a bad testament for a supposedly temporary building. Nissen huts too – in their scores – were taken down and relocated, especially the bigger ones like the dining halls and various mess buildings. Rebuilt to whatever size was required on farms and business premises all over north-east Scotland, they served their purposes as hen-houses and tractor sheds, rotting gently away over the decades until broken and derelict, giving no outward clues to the intense human dramas had had taken place under those rusting tin roofs so many years before.

These stories, and the history behind them all, were soon in just as much danger of slowly dissolving away while the post-war world unfolded. As stated in the introduction, there were a lot of compelling war stories to be told in the fifties and sixties, and it was only due to the huge photographic legacy of Banff Strike Wing that the story occasionally popped into view in the pages of special interest aviation books – most notably those of Chaz Bowyer, although authors like Roy Nesbit and David Smith began to help wave the flag in the early 1980s. A decade before this, however, came a series of events back at the abandoned old airfield, that would see it once more reverberate to the sound of aero engines.

In 1976, after four years of effort by local enthusiasts, Banff airfield was re-opened, this time as a base for leisure aviation in the hands of Banff Flying Club. The main runway was cleared and the control tower refurbished with a lounge, kitchen and toilets. Certifications were obtained and clearances provided, and on the sunny 2 June that year, visiting light aircraft began to arrive at Banff and line up on the secondary runway to await the two main events scheduled for that day. The first, was the return to Banff after 30 years of Sir Max Aitken, who performed an opening ceremony in the control tower by unveiling a plaque. He'd wanted to fly straight into Banff in his personal HS125, until David Morgan, the driving force

THE MEMORY

Last flight from Banff, 13 July 1985: Despite the airfield being closed for flying, the pilot of Cessna Stationair G-BHWW stopped-off here before dropping the Golden Lions *parachute display team over Banff Gala. Here he takes off from runway number three, over one of the big white crosses denoting that the runway is not to be used by aircraft – at least not legally. This was the last time an aircraft ever flew from Banff airfield.*

Flight over Banff –1: Taken from another Cessna by the author in 1986, this photograph shows how little remained of the technical site on the eastern end of the airfield even then. Now, there is even less, and while the pine tree plantation at the top left is now fully grown, the few remaining buildings continue to crumble into the soil.

Flight over Banff – 2: April 1986, and the Cessna camera ship passes over the same frying pan dispersals at the western end of the airfield that can be seen full of Mosquitos in the 1945 photo in Chapter 2. Now, even these impressive wartime artefacts have been ploughed under and have completely disappeared, although the one on the right now hosts a wind turbine.

Ole Inge Lindaas: Former 333 Squadron ground crewman Lindaas hailed from Oslo and worked for the airline SAS. He came back to Banff every year to lay a wreath on the runway and thereby inspired the building of the memorial. Here, he grabs the chance to be seen with Mosquito RR299 at an air display in Oslo – the same Mosquito that he would watch displaying over the newly-unveiled Banff Strike Wing Memorial in September 1989.

THE MEMORY

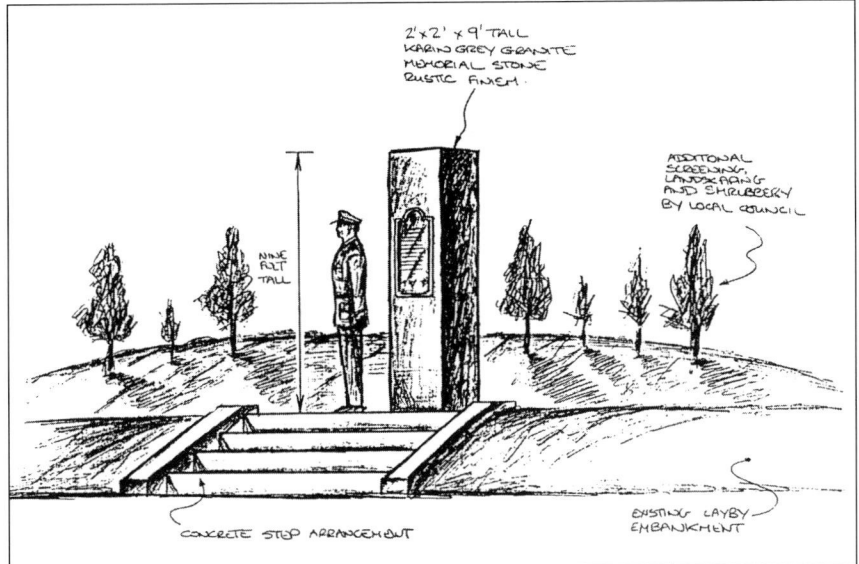

How about this: This sketch by the author of a proposed memorial led to the first and only reunion of Banff Strike Wing veterans on Thursday, 28 September 1989.

behind the flying club project, advised him that the runway was a bit too old and a bit too short to allow a twin-engined executive jet to do this safely.

The second highly anticipated event of the day was the arrival of Neil Williams in the Strathallan Collection's silver-painted Mosquito RS712. Her appearance stirred many hearts that day, not least this writer, who as a 13-year-old schoolboy watched her roar low over the school playing fields at nearby Turriff en-route to Banff, causing two football teams of boys weaned on Airfix kits, to stop and gaze in awe at this incredible sight. The aircraft made a majestic landing and together with the deeply sun-tanned figure of Max Aitken, the photogenic pairing once again rekindled their love affair with the camera.

It would have seemed that these events would at last thrust the history of Banff Strike Wing back into the limelight, but unfortunately it was not to be. The media was far less wall-to-wall than it is today, and the event received only local coverage. Worse, even as the shutters clicked on that opening day, the new flying club was already doomed.

In a word, the problem was money. With the advent of the Middle East oil crisis and the appearance of Sheikh Yamani as the high priest of even higher crude oil prices, the writing was on the wall for the flying club. Pleasure flying suddenly became much too expensive, and few people could afford the increasingly steep cost of the lessons that the club relied on for revenue. Before the decade was out, so too were any hopes of continuing to operate a viable flying club at Banff.

Age shall not weary them: The newly-unveiled memorial to Banff Strike Wing forms a suitable backdrop for a small gathering of the large contingent of veterans who returned to Banff in September 1989 for the ceremony. Among those pictured are Don Lampard, "Puppy" Calder and "Spike" Holly. The DFC (Distinguished Flying Cross) medal was very much in evidence that day, and although it seems hard to associate these smiling elderly men with the images of air combat seen in this book, these nonetheless are some of the people who risked their lives to fight and defeat Hitler. That evening, the hangar doors were pulled wide open.

The gathering: At the memorial unveiling ceremony, former 248 Squadron commander Bill Sise stands in the front row, with Lady Aitken on his left. In front of the senior police officer at the left, is Group Captain Angus McIntosh. Behind, are the ranks of grey-haired veterans of the Strike Wing, who had travelled here from all over the world. Immediately behind the crowd, is the field where Rolf Leithe crashed and died in his Mosquito in 1945.

THE MEMORY

Ready for the flypast: Mosquito display pilot Tony Craig stopped-off at RAF Kinloss, where this photograph was taken, the night before the memorial unveiling ceremony. The following day, the flypasts began with a Nimrod flanked by a couple of Buccaneers. Then Tony joined the Nimrod in the Mosquito, before being let loose on his own with a long and spectacular series of low-level displays over the memorial. Sadly, this very rare airworthy Mosquito was lost with its crew in a tragic crash at an air display on the 21 July 1996.

The Mighty Hunter: The 1989 ceremony was graced by a strong contemporary RAF presence. In addition to a brass band, the RAF laid on two Buccaneers and a Nimrod to join the Mosquito. Here, the Nimrod – appropriately, an anti-submarine aircraft – salutes the memorial before departing to allow the Mosquito to provide an extended display over the ceremony.

The Operations Room Wall – 1945: Although of poor quality, this is the only known contemporary photograph of the wall inside the Operations Block that was painted with the tally-board of ships, aircraft, U-boats and other targets attacked by Banff Strike Wing.

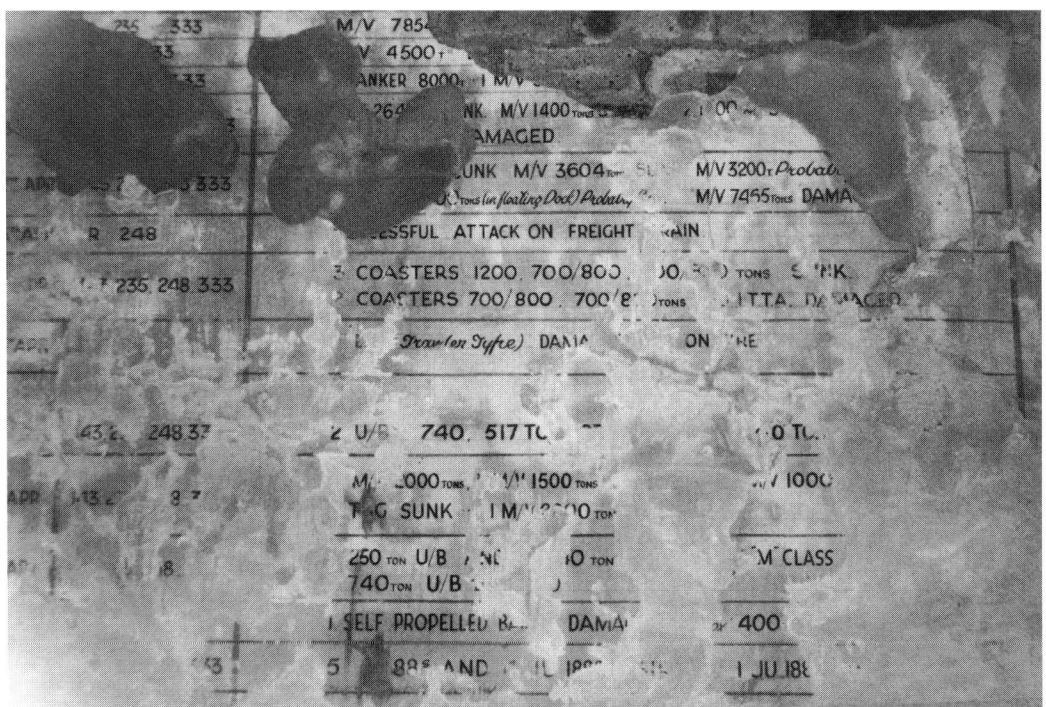

The Operations Room wall – 1985: The author took this photograph of the remnants of the wall in 1985 in order to catalogue and duplicate it. Twenty-five years later, none of it remains – the plaster having been deliberately ripped off the wall by vandals. It is all now a pile of dust.

THE MEMORY

The Operations Block – 2009. Although there are plans to try to preserve it, this remarkable piece of wartime architecture may now in reality be beyond economic repair. Behind can be seen one of the eight (and counting) wind turbines now installed on the old airfield.

Once more, the airfield found itself abandoned and forgotten, and the story might have ended there had it not unwittingly been for an elderly Norwegian gentleman named Ole Inge Lindaas. As a young man, Lindaas had fled his native Norway during World War Two and ended-up in north-east Scotland as a member of the ground crew of the Norwegian 333 Squadron at RAF Banff. Every year since, he'd come back to Banff to pay his respects to those who had fought and died there. His routine rarely varied. Ole worked for the SAS airline in Oslo and could cadge a lift on the scheduled service from Stavanger to Aberdeen whenever he felt like it. Having picked up a hire car at Aberdeen airport, he would proudly drape a large Norwegian flag in the rear window then drive out to Banff.

Following his habitual airfield visit, Ole would then retire to nearby Rowantree Cottage to enjoy a glass or two of SAS duty-free

Still there: This lintel inside the semi-derelict operations block still bears this rather haunting stencilled legend. A veritable time-capsule, this darkened little building never fail to impress those visitors who value such history – though not all visitors have such good intentions.

Silent Witness: This typical example of the much-stencilled walls inside the central briefing room of the Operations Block seems to have survived the vandals and graffiti artists – for now. The lettering tells its own story, although nothing quite makes the spine tingle as much as looking at this remnant of war inside the dark and derelict interior of the ops block itself.

whisky with old Peter Mackenzie. Peter was a crofter who had lived at Rowantree all his life and – true to ancient Scottish tradition – always gave a warm welcome to anyone arriving at his door bearing a bottle of malt whisky. Rowantree was situated near the airfield boundary and in late 1944, Peter had allowed a friendly young Mosquito pilot from 235 Squadron named Flight Lieutenant Douglas to store his Austin car in Peter's barn. Shortly afterwards in January 1945, Peter had watched the young pilot slow-rolling his Mosquito at low level directly over Rowantree. In the dazzling sunshine of a winter day, Douglas had become snow-blinded while inverted and his aircraft plunged into neighbouring Hopetoun cottage and exploded. Douglas, together with ground fitter LAC Robbins who was on the test flight with him, had both died instantly. Two women inside the tiny cottage escaped the inferno of burning petrol and exploding ammunition unhurt through a window. Hopetoun cottage – which can just be seen in the background of the famous *Taxi Rank* photograph – stayed exactly as it had done after the crash until 1987, when it was finally demolished by the landowners. That day, some of us went to have a look. Peter, Ole and myself watched as the propeller blades, undercarriage and live 20mm ammunition from the crashed Mosquito once more saw the light of day. Then Ole quietly performed the task that he always came to Banff to perform – he laid a wreath at the side of one of the runways.

Taxi Rank: This is the perimeter track where the Mosquitos rumbled up the hill towards the runway in the famous wartime photograph – seen here in 2009. Beyond, is the semi-derelict control tower from where the picture was taken, and which Angus McIntosh almost flew into while crash-landing his damaged Mosquito in 1945.

THE MEMORY

When I enquired why, he politely asked me where else I thought he should put it.

That single remark led to the creation of the RAF Banff Strike Wing Memorial Trust, a group dedicated to what was an obvious goal thanks to the name. David Morgan once again threw his considerable energies into my rather naïve idea of building a memorial and within no time we were in business. By September 1989, we found ourselves standing in a large crowd next to our newly unveiled memorial near the old airfield. Following the unveiling, we watched as an RAF Nimrod and two Buccaneers, followed by the last airworthy Mosquito in Britain, performed a series of flypasts and displays to mark the occasion.

Prominent among the watching crowd, was a large contingent of Banff Strike Wing veterans who had travelled from all over the world to be here for the ceremony. There was an entire plane-load from Norway who had flown over in a Royal Norwegian Air Force P-3 Orion aircraft, although for reasons he would never explain to me, Ole felt that he could not be present at the ceremony, and instead watched the Mosquito display while standing alone on a runway up on the airfield itself. The memorial was unveiled by the senior surviving member of the Strike Wing, Bill Sise, who had travelled from New Zealand. Our own trust chairman, the magnificent Group Captain Angus McIntosh from Edinburgh, presided over the proceedings. Sadly, the great Sir Max Aitken had died four years earlier, although his widow Lady Aitken came along to the ceremony. All of the six squadrons who at one time or another had constituted the Banff Strike Wing were represented, even the Canadians of 404 Squadron, who had also come a long way and were as irrepressible as ever. One 235 squadron veteran, also from Canada,

Father and Son: A treasured snapshot from Bill Atkinson shows him as a baby with his father, Wing Commander Richard Atkinson, DSO, DFC, in October 1944 at Distillery Cottages, Inverboyndie. They would be destined never to know each other when Dick was killed shortly after this picture was taken, on the 13 December 1944 over Askvoll in Norway.

> **"IN FEAR AND TREMBLING"**
> Members of the Officers Mess were glad about the (VE Day) bonfire. The first time they have been warm since they got here. The Fire Section have never had so much fun. It got all its equipment working at once. And it worked, it worked! Even if it could not be stopped.
> *Chocks Away, Victory Edition, May 1945*

the still game and endlessly exuberant "Puppy" Calder, had flown in combat operations from both Banff and Dallachy airfields. He thoroughly enjoyed handing out his personal card to everyone he met, which read:

Puppy Calder: No Job, No Money, No Prospects - No Worries.

For one brief moment that September the veterans of Banff Strike Wing – from WAAFs and ground crews to pilots and navigators – were together again, back among their comrades at the place where their youth had burned so brightly in those years of wartime. All had donated so generously to the cause, even if many of them were no longer able to manage the trip to Banff any more, and it is fair to say that the bulk of the £30,000 needed to build the memorial came from these Strike Wing veterans themselves.

Following the unveiling ceremony, a social get-together was planned to take place at a local hotel in the evening. Puppy Calder warned me that the "hangar doors would be wide open" at this event, and that we were in for "lots of line shooting." They were, and we got it – but then again, we were suckers for it all anyway. These people were talking about events many of us could hardly imagine, let alone take part in. Brought together like this for the first time in almost fifty years, their memories were suddenly refreshed. Tony Gadd was asked almost as many questions about filming *The Shipbusters* documentary as his part in the real thing. Ron Brooks from 248 Squadron met Angus McIntosh for the first time since "you came back with that bloody great hole in your wing and nearly wiped out the control tower." Angus had been elected as a suitably distinguished chairman of the charitable trust we set up to raise the funds needed to build the memorial. From his fellow trustees, he was presented that evening (to lots of ribbing from other former Mosquito pilots) with

"The heart knows more than monuments can raise": *Sharing a private moment of remembrance at Ejdsfjord, Askvoll, Norway in 2007 is Bill Atkinson, with his son Job and Aud Kari Steinsland, the Mayor of Askvoll. They gaze at the spot where Bill's father Dick Atkinson and his navigator Val Upton, crashed and died after being hit by German flak.*

THE MEMORY

a superb scale model diorama of his Mosquito lying crashed and broken on the grass at RAF Banff in 1945.

Characters and former pilots like the wonderful "Johnny" Johanssen from 333 Squadron mingled with people like David Pitkeathly from 235 Squadron, who took along his "dog collar" to prove that he really was now *The Reverend* Pitkeathly. Max Aitken's widow Lady Aitken mingled easily with scores of former station personnel, while journalists and reporters rushed around gathering stories and interviews. The gathering was a unique one in the true sense of the word. Squadron associations had formed and met regularly, but this was the one and only time that Banff Strike Wing itself had ever been fully reunited.

The events of that day attracted a lot of media coverage, some of it exactly what the history of Banff Strike Wing needed. Historical aviation magazines had become very popular by then, and the coverage received from them seemed to really kick-start a lot of wider interest in the subject. Soon, there were articles and books about the Strike Wing coming from all directions, as well as paintings of Strike Wing scenes and even collectors editions of die-cast Banff Mosquitos. It seems reasonable to suggest that not only had we created a memorial, but also a wider upsurge of interest in the story of Banff Strike Wing as well. Their history is now safe, and better known than it has ever been.

The airfield, meantime, continues to slowly crumble back into the soil. The natural reaction of enthusiasts and relatives of former personnel who visit it, is always one of concern that it should be preserved. But should it, and indeed, could it be?

The question of whether it *could* be preserved is debatable. Today, there is less money available than ever to undertake preservation work. At the time of writing, a local trust is being set up to try to preserve the former Operations Block. Yet in 1987, this writer undertook a full dimensional survey of the building in order to transfer the details on to a modern CAD drawing. Even then, the fabric of the building was in a poor state, but at least it was still structurally sound. Twenty years later, another limited survey revealed a much more severe level of deterioration and even some subsidence. No longer is refurbishment realistically feasible. Stabilisation of the ruin is perhaps the best that can now be hoped for this unique wartime building. In order to allow future generations to see what this building was like in its heyday, perhaps the answer is to build an exact replica, in a more accessible location, which would be considerably cheaper than trying to repair and maintain the original.

The less obvious answer to the question of whether the airfield *should* be preserved, is that actually, it has been. Or rather, it has not been obliterated, like so many wartime airfields have. Yes, most of the buildings have gone, but then that was always the intention – the place was never intended to be anything other than a temporary wartime facility. Some areas now host large-scale agricultural buildings, and a go-karting club has been at the airfield for some forty years, but on the whole, most of the airfield remains exactly as it was when the war ended. Some of the frying pan dispersals have been covered over and removed, while the runways get a little narrower year by year. Yet the sheer amount of concrete that would have to be removed means the airfield will still exist for many more decades to come.

Much more significantly, the fact that the airfield has now been turned into a wind farm, with eight huge turbines scattered across it, has actually *guaranteed* the continued preservation that comes

"EDITORIAL – THE TWENTIETH CENTURY"
By Flight Lieutenant G.R. Mayhew, DFC.

History, being discovered in the next decade, is unobserved by those who make it or are present at its inception. The worth of events is put too often upon their immediate effect. Circumstances which prove auspicious are at their moment thought ordinary, actions which are hailed with acclamation prove no more resounding than a firework.

The world of our time has had a poor contemporary judgement. Since the turn of the century events which have in succession threatened the pockets, the larders, the jobs and finally the lives of millions of people the world over have not commended themselves as favourable omens. A great number of people have come to the terrible conclusion that the meagre benefits of life do not make worthwhile the struggle, poverty and mental imprisonment they require. They say the world is no fit place to bring new life into.

But, averse as have been the years before, they have seen the actions which may finally, strange though it may sound to us, call this the Century of Progress.

Twice the world has faced domination by despotic powers – and twice they have been overwhelmed by the forces that once appeared to need only a finishing blow. Two men, Hitler, whose record for cruelty and oppression for evil ends has been the worst that mankind has known, and Mussolini, who put into practise the base ideal that man is born not to serve the community but the state, have risen to unparalleled power – and have been beaten more completely than any other animal of their kind has been.

The years which have seen the worst terrors of mankind have also seen their utter defeat. Such victories in war cannot be dishonoured by defeat in peace. From such harsh beginnings a great future may be made.

Chocks Away, Victory Edition, May 1945

THE MEMORY

from simply being left alone. Better still, the windfarm company has now funded the first direct pedestrian access onto the airfield, via a car park at the Boyndie Day Centre, where a display of Banff Strike Wing memorabilia and photographs has been established by the Banff Airfield Association. With this new pathway, together with Scotland's recent *Right to Roam* legislation, access to this historic old airfield has never been easier nor more lawful, and this combination now surely has real tourist potential for aviation and history enthusiasts, not to mention schools and other groups – if only for walking around and looking at the way things once were.

So long as the control tower can be left safely standing – now guaranteed by being formally listed – it is still possible to go up onto the balcony and look at the scene of the 1945 *Taxi Rank* photograph and see it essentially as it was then, slightly desolate and windswept, but with a brooding, palpable sense of history about it all, and with that distinctive perimeter track still curving away into the distance. From April 1943 onwards, this quiet coastal hillside became - and now thankfully always will be – a very photogenic place.

Get the camera out, and you may just capture a classic moment in time.

One last look: The location of the famous 1945 Taxi Rank *photograph, as seen from the control tower in the spring of 1985. Despite the absence of the huts and the hangars and the people and the planes, the landscape is an unmistakable one. The control tower still stands at the time of writing, and this view can still be witnessed – although with added windmills.*

Appendix 1

BANFF STRIKE WING ROLL OF HONOUR

(Compiled by Group Captain Angus McIntosh, 1989)

This listing does not include non-fatal incidents such as crash-landings, captured crews and internments.

	DATE	AIRCRAFT	PILOT	NAVIGATOR	LOCATION
1	14-9-44	O / 404	Fg. Off. J.M.A. Baribeau (POW)	Flt. Lt. C.H. Taylor	Kristiansand
2	19-9-44	L / 144	FS.R.E.C. Hossack	WO B.C. Wicks	Askevold
3	2-10-44	Q / 404	Fg. Off. E.R. Davey	Fg. Off. L.E.E. Robinson	Wellhead Farm, Portsoy
4	2-10-44	E / 404	Fg. Off. G.A. Long	Fg. Off. F.M. Stickel	Wellhead Farm, Portsoy
5	13-10-44	K / 248	Flt. Lt. G.E. Nicholls	Fg. Off. A. Hanson	Utsire / Kristiansand
6	19-10-44	F / 235	WO N.M.M. Martin	WO I.L. Ramsay (POW)	Askvoll
7	21-10-44	I / 248	Fg. Off. R.S. Driscoll	Fg. Off. T.A. Hannant	Haugesund
8	28-10-44	P / 235	Fg. Off J.T. Ross	Fg. Off. F.L. Walker	RAF Banff
9	4-11-44	L / 235	Fg. Off. H.L. Powell	Fg. Off. N.L. Redford	Kinn
10	5-12-44	P / 143	Fg. Off. R. Gilchrist	Fg. Off. W. Knight (injured)	RAF Sumburgh
11	5-12-44	G / 248	Flt. Lt. L.N. Collins	Fg. Off. R.H. Hurn	Nordgulen
12	7-12-44	O / 248	Fg. Off. W.N. Cosman	Fg. Off. L.M. Freedman	Gossen
13	7-12-44	Z / 248	Fg. Off. K. C. Wing	Plt. Off V. R. Shield	Gossen
14	13-12-44	R / 235	Wg. Cdr. R.A. Atkinson	Fg. Off. V.C. Upton	Eidsfjord, Askvoll
15	16-12-44	R / 248	Flt. Lt. J. Kennedy	Fg. Off. W. Rolls	Kraakhellesund
16	16-12-44	S / 235	Fg. Off. K.C. Beruldsen	Plt. Off. T.D.S. Rabbitts	Losnoy, near Gulen
17	21-12-44	HR284/248	Plt. Off. W.D. Livock	FS. G.L. West	Covesea, Lossiemouth
18	26-12-44	G / 235	Fg. Off. E.J. Fletcher	Fg. Off. A.J. Watson	Leirvik
18	31-12-44	U / 248	Flt. Lt. J.F. Lown	Fg. Off. C.J. Daynton	Flekkefjord
20	9-1-45	HR159/235	Flt. Lt. D.B. Douglas	LAC G.P. Robbins	Hopetoun, RAF Banff
21	11-1-45	M / 143	FS. P.C.L. Smoolenaers	FS. W. Harris	Flekkefjord
22	15-1-45	K / 143	Cdt. M.J.M. Guedj aka "Maurice"	Flt. Lt. J.E. Langley	Leirvik
23	15-1-45	D / 143	FS. G.A. Morton-Moncrieff	FS. C. Cash	Leirvik
24	15-1-45	V / 143	Lt. F.E. Alexandre (USAAF)	Plt. Off. J. A. McMullin	Leirvik

APPENDIX 1

25	15-1-45	A / 235	FS. F. Chew	FS. S.W. Couttie (POW)	Leirvik
26	15-1-45	R / 333	Q/M K. Sjolie	Q/M J.S. Gausland	Leirvik
27	25-1-45	F / 248	Flt. Lt. D.S.L. Crimp	Fg. Off. J. Bird	Roughilly Wood, Portsoy
28	29-1-45	N/65 (Mustang)	Sqn. Ldr. I.D.S. Strachan	-	North Sea
29	24-2-45	RF603/248	Flt. Lt. L.R. Bacon	Fg. Off. W. M. Miller	Macduff Golf Course
30	7-3-45	O / 235	Fg. Off S.C. Hawkins	Fg. Off. E. Stubbs	Kattegat
31	7-3-45	R / 248	Flt Lt. R.G. Young	Fg. Off. G.V. Goodes	Kattegat
32	11-3-45	N / 333	Lt. R. Almton	Sub. Lt. P. Hjorthen	Haugesund
33	12-3-45	Q / 248	WO. R.W. Moffatt	Fg. Off. B.A.S. Abbott	Skaggerak
34	17-3-45	F / 143	Fg. Off. W.J. Ceybird	Flt. Lt. N. Harwood	Aalesund
35	22-3-45	K / 333	Lt. R. Leithe	Sub. Lt. N. Skfelanger (injured)	RAF Banff
36	23-3-45	W / 235	Sqn. Ldr. R. Reid	Fg. Off. A.D. Turner	Dalsafjord
37	23-3-45	R / 143	Plt. Off. K. McCall	WO. J.A. Etchells	Tejgenaes
38	24-3-45	Q / 235	Flt. Lt. J. R. Williams	Flt. Lt. J.T. Flower	Helliso
39	25-3-45	V / 248	Flt. Lt. A. McLeod	WO. N. Wheeley	Vilnes Fjord
40	25-3-45	G / 333	Flt. Cdr. K. Skavhaugen	Flg. Off. A.H. Bobbett	Vilnes Fjord
41	30-3-45	T / 235	Flt. Lt. W. Knowles	FS. L. Thomas	Porsgrunn-Skien
42	5-4-45	Y / 235	Plt. Off. L.E. Arthars	FS. F.G. Richardson	Anholt, Kattegat
43	9-4-45	DZ592	Flt. Lt. W.M.O. Jones (Film Unit)	Fg. Off. A.J. Newell (Film Unit)	Kattegat
44	11-4-45	H / 333	Sub. Lt. J.W. Loken	Sgt. S.H. Engstrom	Porsgrunn
45	19-4-45	V / 235	FS. A.R. McKenzie	FS. F.A. Relfe	Jutland, Denmark
46	4/5/45	RS568	Flt. Lt. D.K. Thorburn	WO. L.W.R. Crocker (injured)	Varburg, Sweden

Appendix 2

SHIPS SUNK BY BANFF STRIKE WING

Name	Type	Tonnage	Location	Date
Sulldorf Vp1608	Flak Ship	264	Kristiansand	14-9-44
F. Suthmeir Vp1202	Flak Ship	194	Heligoland	17-9-44
Lynx	Merchant	1364	Askevold	19-9-44
Tyrifjord	Merchant	3080	Askevold	19-9-44
Vangsnes	Merchant	191	Lister	21-9-44
Hygia	Merchant	104	Lister	21-9-44
-	Armed Trawler	75	Lister	21-9-44
Biber V5502	Harbour defence	168	Hjeltefjord.	24-9-44
Rudolf Oldendorff	Merchant	1953	Egersund	9-10-44
O.T. Anderson Uj.1711	Sub Chaser	485	Egersund	9-10-44
Inger Johanne	Tanker	1202	Kristiansand	15-10-44
Mosel Vp1605	Flak ship	426	Kristiansand	15-10-44
Eckenheim	Merchant	1923	Haugesund	21-10-44
Vestra	Merchant	1432	Haugesund	21-10-44
Zick V5506	Harbour vessel	220	Hjeltefjord	23-10-44
R32	R-Boat	110	Rekefjord	13-11-44
529	Rescue Boat	75	Rekefjord	13-11-44
Sardinien	Armed Trawler	177	Sognefjord	14-11-44
Gudrun	Merchant	1485	Flekkefjord	10-12-44
Wartheland	Merchant	3678	Ejdfjord	12-10-44
Ferndale	Merchant	5684	Kraakhellesund.	16-12-44
Parat	Tug	135	Kraakhellesund.	16-12-44
La France	Merchant	617	Skudesnes.	28-12-44
Palermo	Merchant	1461	Flekkefjord	31-12-44
Achilles	Merchant	998	Flekkefjord	31-12-44
Seehund VP5304	Flak Ship	320	Leirvik	15-1-45
Ilse Fritzen	Merchant	5099	Edjfjord & Malloy	25-1-45

APPENDIX 2

Bjergfin	Merchant	696	Edjfjord & Malloy	25-1-45
Austri	Merchant	490	Leirvik	21-2-45
4 x un-named	Gun Barges	520	Kattegat	7-3-45
Iris	Merchant	3323	Aalesund	17-3-45
Remage	Merchant	1830	Aalesund	17-3-45
Log	Merchant	1684	Aalesund	17-3-45
Lysaker	Merchant	910	Aalesund/Dalsafjord	23-3-45
Scharnhorn	Merchant	2643	Porsgrunn-Skien	30-3-45
Gudrid Borgstad	Merchant	1664	Porsgrunn-Skien	30-3-45
Svanefjell	Merchant	1371	Porsgrunn-Skien	30-3-45
Gudrid	Merchant	1305	Porsgrunn-Skien	30-3-45
Torafire	Merchant	823	Porsgrunn-Skien	30-3-45
Concordia	Merchant	5154	Sandefjord	2-4-45
William Blumer	Merchant	3604	Sandefjord	2-4-45
Helmi Sohle	Flak Ship	453	Kattegat	5-4-45
–	Armed Trawler	50	Kattegat	5-4-45
U-804	Type IXC U-Boat	1144	Kattegat	9-4-45
U-843	Type IXC U-Boat	1120	Kattegat	9-4-45
U-1065	Type VIIC U-Boat	769	Kattegat	9-4-45
Dione	Merchant	1620	Porsgrunn-Skien	11-4-45
Kalmar	Merchant	964	Porsgrunn-Skien	11-4-45
Nordsjo	Merchant	178	Porsgrunn-Skien	11-4-45
Traust	Merchant	190	Porsgrunn-Skien	11-4-45
U-521	Type VIIC U-Boat	769	Kattegat	19-4-45
U-2359	Type XXIII U-Boat	234	Kattegat	2-5-45
M-293	Minesweeper	637	Kattegat	2-5-45
Wolfgang L.M. Russ	Merchant	3750	Kattegat	4-5-45

Appendix 3

FORMER BANFF STRIKE WING PERSONNEL, CORRESPONDENCE AND INTERVIEWS

143 SQUADRON
Brown, David
Carr, Norman

144 SQUADRON
Andrew, John M.
Boorer, Bill
Brett, Peter
Fuld, R.H.
Gadd, Tony
Gribbin, Jim
Harrison, Ray
Holly, F.S. "Spike"
Lampard, Don
Marrow, Duncan
Mitchell, A.M.
Reeves, D.E
Rogers, Don
Thurgood, Alf

235 SQUADRON
Armstrong, Tom
Brown, E.C.
Bowden, Geoffrey L.
Burton, Ron
Calder, J.M. "Puppy"
Elliot, Kenneth
Frost, D, "Jack"
Gogswell, C.A.
Hill, Frank G.
Jackson, Arthur
Pitkeathly, Rev. D.
Roe, Bob
Rix, Alex
Shield, D.M.
Siddons, Fred W.
Strachan, Adam
Williamson, Alec

248 SQUADRON
Brooks, Ron T.
Earnshaw, Norman
Gittins, E.
McIntosh, Angus
Montagu-Smith, A.
Nicholson, Harold
Parfitt, Bill
Peters, Alan D.
Price, Ray
Scott, T.C.
Sise, Bill
Voce, R.A. (Bill)
Woodcock, W.G

333 (NORWEGIAN) SQUADRON
Johansen, Egil D.
Lindaas, Ole Inge

404 CANADIAN SQUADRON
Basset, P.
Carlin, James
Cummins, John. S.
Faithfull, Dr. S.T.
Goring, Lloyd M.
Johnsson, Ivar
McCamus, WH 'Mac'
Stoddart, J.R.E.
Watlington, H.F.

WAAF
Bryson, Margaret
Day, Rachel
Denholm, Violet
Hickey, Joy
Sherlock, Joyce

BIBLIOGRAPHY AND SOURCES

BOOKS

Action Stations Number 7, David J. Smith
Patrick Stephens Ltd, Cambridge, 1983

Armageddon, Max Hastings
Macmillan, London, 2004

Beaufighter at War, Chaz Bowyer
Ian Allan, London, 1976

Boys of Spring, The. G. Gordon Symons.
Self-Published by the Author, Canada, 2006

Coastal Command at War, Chaz Bowyer
Ian Allan, London, 1979

Dangerous Sky, The. Tom Coughlin
The Ryserson Press, Toronto, 1968

Fraserburgh at War, George Allan Dey
BCP-AUP, Aberdeen, 1990

Hell on High Ground, David W. Earl
Airlife Publishing Ltd, Suffolk, 1999

History of the RAF, Chaz Bowyer
The Hamlyn Publishing Group Ltd, Middlesex, 1977

Last Year of the Luftwaffe, Alfred Price
Wren's Park Publishing, London, 1999

Lighter Shade of Blue, A. C. Foxley-Norris.
Ian Allan Ltd, Shepperton, Surrey, 1978

Luftwaffe Data Book, Alfred Price
Greenhill Books, London, 1997

Luftwaffe over Scotland, Les Taylor
Whittles Publishing, Wick, UK, 2010

Making of Modern Britain, The. Andrew Marr.
Macmillan, London, 2009.

Mosquito at War, Chaz Bowyer
Ian Allan, London, 1973

Mosquito Fighter Bomber Units 1942-1945, Martin Bowman
Osprey Publishing Ltd, Oxford 1998

Mosquito Fighter Squadrons – In Focus, Philip Birtles
Red Kite Books, Surrey, 2005

Mosquito in Action, Part 2, Jerry Scutts.
Squadron Signal Publications, Texas, USA, 1993

Mosquito Squadrons of the Royal Air Force, Chaz Bowyer
Ian Allan Publishing, London, 1984

Phoenix Triumphant, E.R. Hooton
Arms and Armour Press, London, 1994

Scandinavian Sideshow 1940-1945, Various Authors,
Osprey Aviation, Oxford, 2000

Scotland at War, Ian Nimmo
Archive Publications Ltd, Cheshire, 1989

Scotland's War, Seona Robertson & Les Wilson
Mainstream Publishing, Edinburgh, 1995

Separate Little War, A. Andrew D. Bird.
Grub Street, London, 2006

Steep Turn to the Stars, A, Jim Hughes
Benevenagh Book, Elgin, UK, 1981.

Strike Wings, The. Roy Conyers Nesbit
William Kimber, London, 1984

Wings of the Luftwaffe. Eric Brown
Pilot Press Ltd, London, 1977

Why the Allies Won, Richard Overy
Pimlico, London, 1995

DOCUMENTS AND ARTICLES

Ace from the Auxiliaries (Max Aitken)
Wings Encyclopaedia of Aviation, Orbis Publishing, London, 1977

Banff: Aviation Archaeology, David Smith
Flypast Magazine, Key Publishing, Stamford, UK, December 1984

Banff Strike Wing Memorial Project 1987-1989, Les Taylor
Banff Strike Wing Memorial Trust, 1989.

Banff Strike Wing Roll of Honour, Gp.Cpt. A. McIntosh, DFC
RAF Banff Strike Wing Memorial Trust, 1989.

Banffshire Journal, Archives, 1944-1945.
Macduff Public Library, 17 High Street, Macduff, Banffshire

Black Monday (Leirvik Air Battle), Halvor Sperbund
Flypast Magazine, Key Publishing, Stamford UK, March 2001

Carve Their Names With Pride, David Morgan
Banffshire Journal, 15 September 1987.

Cold Water Immersion Effects, Survival at Sea.
RGIT Offshore Survival Centre, Aberdeen, 1983.

Ein Son Sitt Siste Oppdrag (Bill Atkinson), Ingunn Osland
Fjordalangs, Forde, Norge, May 2007

Emmaville to Askvoll, Bill Atkinson
Atkinson Family Private Publication, 1989.

Flyers Rain Death from Limelit Sky over A Night Sea, Carl Olsson,
Illustrated, London, 27 January 1945.

Group Captain "Bill" Sise, Obituaries.
Daily Telegraph, London, 18 February 2004

RAF Banff Strike Wing (DVD), David Morgan.
Banff Strike Wing Association, 2008.

Rocket Terror of The Fjords, Sqn/Ldr. William Simpson, DFC
Sunday Express, London, 14 February 1945

Strategic Air War Against Germany, 1939-1945, Sebastian Cox.
British Bombing Survey Unit, Frank Cass Publishers 1998

Various Squadron and Station Operations Books.
Public Record Office/National Archives, Kew, London

ONLINE SOURCES

Aviation History Society, Norway - www.ahs.no
Axis History Forum - forum.axishistory.com
Feldgrau – Research on German Armed Forces - www.feldgrau.com
Luftwaffe in Norway, Special Interest Group - www.luftwaffe.no/bilde2.html
Luftwaffe Archives & Records Resource Group - www.lwag.org
Luftwaffe Data - luftwaffedata.co.uk
Luftwaffe, 1933-1945 - www.ww2.dk
Secret Scotland - www.secretscotland.org.uk
Twelve O'clock High - forum.12oclockhigh.net
U-Boat Net – uboat.net
Wartime Memories Project - www.wartimememories.co.uk
World War Two Airfields & Radar Stations - worldwar2airfields.fotopic.net
WW2 in Color Forum - www.ww2incolor.com